ACCOUNT OF THE FABLES AND RITES OF THE INCAS

THE WILLIAM & BETTYE NOWLIN SERIES
in Art, History, and Culture of the Western Hemisphere

Account of the Fables and Rites of the Incas

BY CRISTÓBAL DE MOLINA

WITH AN INTRODUCTION BY BRIAN S. BAUER
TRANSLATED AND EDITED BY
BRIAN S. BAUER
VANIA SMITH-OKA
GABRIEL E. CANTARUTTI

University of Texas Press ◄◊► Austin

Requests for permission to reproduce material from this work should be sent to:
Permissions
University of Texas Press
P.O. Box 7819
Austin, TX 78713-7819
www.utexas.edu/utpress/about/bpermission.html

∞ The paper used in this book meets the minimum requirements of
ANSI/NISO Z39.48-1992 (R1997) (Permanence of Paper).

LIBRARY OF CONGRESS CATALOGING-IN-PUBLICATION DATA
Molina, Cristóbal de, 16th cent.
[Relación de las fábulas y ritos de los Incas. English]
Account of the fables and rites of the Incas / by Cristóbal de Molina ; with an
introduction by Brian S. Bauer ; translated and edited by Brian S. Bauer, Vania
Smith-Oka, Gabriel E. Cantarutti.
p.   cm. — (The William and Bettye Nowlin series in art, history, and culture
of the Western Hemisphere)
Includes bibliographical references and index.
ISBN 978-0-292-72383-2 (cloth : alk. paper)
1. Inca mythology.   2. Peru—History—Conquest, 1522–1548.   I. Bauer, Brian S.
II. Smith-Oka, Vania, 1975–   III. Cantarutti, Gabriel E.   IV. Title.
F3429.M7213 2011   299.8′113—dc22   2010045473

ISBN 978-0-292-72999-5 (E-book)

CONTENTS

PREFACE: Translators' Notes vii

Acknowledgments x

The Life and Times of Cristóbal de Molina xi

Introduction *Brian S. Bauer* xiv

Account of the Fables and Rites of the Incas

CHAPTER 1: Introduction 3

CHAPTER 2: Origin Myths 4

CHAPTER 3: Of *Quipus* and Inca Yupanqui 14

CHAPTER 4: The Sorcerers 18

CHAPTER 5: The Rituals of the Months of the Year 21

CHAPTER 6: The *Ayuscay*, *Rutuchico*, and *Quicochico* Rituals 75

CHAPTER 7: The Capacocha 77

CHAPTER 8: Taqui Onqoy 84

APPENDIX: Editions of Cristóbal de Molina's *Account of the Fables and Rites of the Incas* (*Relación de las fábulas y ritos de los incas*) 91

Notes 93

Glossary 123

Bibliography 133

Index 145

Preface

TRANSLATORS' NOTES

*T*he original version of Cristóbal de Molina's manuscript titled *Relación de las fábulas y ritos de los incas* is lost. The only remaining copy is held in the National Library in Madrid (Manuscript 3169, fols. 2–36). The document is not dated, but the handwriting appears to be from the late sixteenth or early seventeenth century (Porras Barrenechea 1986: 353). It is the first of six critically important early colonial works on the Incas that have been bound together with vellum into a single volume (Duviols and Itier 1993: 15). This collection comes from the personal library of Francisco de Ávila (ca. 1573–1647), a Jesuit who led a series of brutal anti-idolatry campaigns in the Andes a generation after Molina. Ávila was also a great collector of books and manuscripts, accruing what then was the largest library in Peru (Salomon 2008; Hampe Martínez 1996). The other documents included in the volume are: Joan de Santa Cruz Pachacuti Yamqui Salcamaygua's *Relación de antigüedades deste reyno del Pirú* (ca. 1613), Polo de Ondegardo's *Traslado de un cartapacio a manera de borrador* (ca. 1572), Francisco de Ávila's *Tratado y relación de los errores, falsos dioses y otras supersticiones* (ca. 1608), the anonymous *Huarochirí Manuscript* (ca. 1608), as well as a summary of Garcilaso de la Vega's *Comentarios reales de los incas* (1609). This famous collection of documents was first identified by Pascual de Gayangos, who sent a copy to Clements R. Markham (1873: vii).

Although we have tried to remain true to Molina throughout this translation, we have made some changes to make his document more accessible to a wide readership. For example, we have divided many of his excessively long sentences into shorter, more comprehensible lengths, and we have added punctuation where it lends clarity to the text. We have also followed English rules of capitalization; spelled out abbreviations included in the manuscript; and added chapter breaks, chapter titles, and subheads that are not present in the original. In some sentences, we have made minor grammatical changes such as correcting tenses and plurals. Furthermore, we have simplified some of the repetitive phrases Molina uses; for example, "*el dicho*" (the said) is generally translated as "that." In far fewer places, we have added a word or two or a proper name to rectify an ambiguous sentence or to clarify confusing pronouns. The added words are marked with square brackets. Finally, we have also simplified some of his sentences by adding commas to separate items in a series and reducing the number of articles.

Some information was noted in the margins of the manuscript. The paragraph breaks were marked with a "v," and various lines of text that contain blank spaces were marked with an "o." These markings have not been reproduced in this translation. However, the other annotative information included in the margins of the document is provided in the footnotes of this translation.[1] Finally, in a few places, words were crossed out and replaced with corrections, and in other passages one or two words were erroneously copied twice. We have reproduced these elements of the text within our translation.

QUECHUA WORDS

Molina's frequent use of Quechua words and his inclusion of numerous Quechua prayers offer great challenges to any publication of his work. The fact that the original document has been lost, and the oldest remaining example of the document is a copy, adds complexities to understanding the Quechua words included within the text. Additional difficulties are introduced when the same Quechua words are spelled in different ways within the manuscript.[2] As our English translation is intended for a general readership, we have standardized the most common toponyms and the names of Inca lords to match the generalized Hispanic spelling as found in other Spanish chronicles and on modern maps. For example, we use Cajamarca not Caxamarca, Huanacauri not Guanacauri or Yanacauri, Vilcabamba not Uiscabamba, Haucaypata not Aucaypata, Inca not Inga, and Manco Capac not Mango Capac.[3] We have, however, followed Molina's spelling for the more obscure terms, places, and names, and we have not attempted to edit his Quechua prayers.

Initially we made our own transcriptions of Molina's Quechua words based on our readings of the Madrid document. We were, however, uneasy with the results of our work, since we are not linguists nor are we Quechua speakers. Fortunately, as we entered into the final stages of our translation work, Julio Calvo Pérez and Henrique Urbano (2008) published a comprehensive paleographic edition of Molina's document. Respecting their fine scholarship, we defer in most cases to their paleographic reading of the document.

After much debate, we have also decided to provide a translation of most Quechua words when they appear in the text. Again, we were hesitant to do this because of our limited Quechua skills, but in the end we believe that in-text translations will help general readers better understand the document. However, to avoid clutter, we translate frequently used words, such as *ayllo* [kin group], *chicha* [an alcoholic drink made from maize], *huaca* [shrine], *mitimas* [colonists], *mullu* [*Spondylus* shells], *taqui* [dance], *tarpuntaes* [priests of the Sun], only on their first use. A general glossary is also provided to help readers understand the many Quechua terms and the wide range of spellings found in the manuscript. Readers who are interested in learning more about the use of Quechua in Molina's work should see Calvo Pérez and Urbano (2008) and other earlier editions of the document.

ACKNOWLEDGMENTS

We thank the Office of the Dean (College of Liberal Arts and Sciences) as well as the Department of Anthropology at the University of Illinois at Chicago for providing financial support for this work. We would also like to thank John Monaghan, Alan Covey, Nancy Warrington, and Jeffrey R. Parsons, who aided us at various stages of the project.

THE LIFE AND TIMES OF
CRISTÓBAL DE MOLINA

CA. 1529   Cristóbal de Molina is born in Baeza, Spain.

1556   Molina arrives in Cuzco.

1558–1560   Polo de Ondegardo's first term as chief magistrate of Cuzco

1564   Luis de Olivera, while serving as the priest of Parinacocha, notes an increase in the idolatrous activities of his parishioners. This movement becomes known as the Taqui Onqoy.

1565   Molina is appointed as the priest in the Hospital for the Natives of Our Lady of Succor in Cuzco. Over time, he was also named preacher general of the Cuzco parishes and visitor general for parts of the Cuzco bishopric.

1568–1571+   Cristóbal de Albornoz leads a series of campaigns in the Peruvian highlands to identify and destroy native shrines and to punish the individuals and communities who worshipped them. Both Molina and Olivera are also active in the anti–idolatry campaigns.

1571   Viceroy Francisco de Toledo meets Albornoz in the Huamanga area.

1571–1572   Toledo is in Cuzco. He orders a series of interviews to be conducted concerning the history of the Incas. Molina writes his now-lost work *History of the Incas* at the request of the viceroy.

1 MARCH 1572   Pedro Sarmiento de Gamboa finishes his *History of the Incas* while in Cuzco.

24 SEPTEMBER 1572   The last independent royal Inca, Tupac Amaru, is executed in Cuzco. Molina is one of several priests who accompany him during his final day.

4 JULY 1573   Sebastián de Lartaún is installed as the third bishop of Cuzco. Soon afterward, Molina provides the bishop with a document titled *Account of the Huacas* as well as a copy of his own *History of the Incas*.

1573/1575?   Molina writes his *Account of the Fables and Rites of the Incas* at the request of Bishop Lartaún.

6 NOVEMBER 1575   While in Arequipa, Toledo orders a salary adjustment for Molina. In his letter, Toledo notes that Molina had collected information on the rites and ceremonies of the Incas.

14 JANUARY 1577   Molina testifies in Cuzco on behalf of Albornoz.

2 APRIL 1582   Molina is interviewed in Cuzco concerning the laws of the Incas.

1582–1583   The Third Lima Provincial Council. Molina attends, but the exact dates are not known. He leaves Cuzco in late May or early June, carrying a letter from the indigenous leaders of Cuzco requesting tax-exempt status. He leaves early, and on his return, Molina meets Albornoz, who was traveling to Lima to attend the council.

9 OCTOBER 1583	Lartaún dies in Lima while attending the Third Lima Provincial Council.
28 MARCH 1584	Molina testifies in Cuzco for the second time on behalf of Albornoz.
29 MAY 1585	Molina dies in Cuzco, at approximately fifty-six years of age.
1586	Miguel Cabello Valboa finishes his *Miscelánea antártica*. He notes that he used Molina's *History of the Incas* while writing the work.
1647	Francisco de Ávila dies. In his enormous library is the only surviving copy of Molina's *Account of the Fables and Rites of the Incas*.
1649	Dean Vasco de Contreras y Valverde finishes his work *Account of the City of Cuzco*. He notes that he used Molina's *History of the Incas* while writing the work.
1653	Bernabé Cobo finishes his work *History of the New World*. He notes that he used Molina's *Account of the Fables and Rites of the Incas*. Cobo's copy of the account is now lost.
1873	Avila's copy of Molina's *Account of the Fables and Rites of the Incas* is found in the National Library in Madrid. Clements Markham publishes an English translation.
1913	The first Spanish edition of Molina's account is published in Chile. Numerous other editions follow.

Brian S. Bauer

INTRODUCTION

his is an English translation of Cristóbal de Molina's manuscript titled *Account of the Fables and Rites of the Incas* (*Relación de las fábulas y ritos de los incas*). Written around 1575 at the request of the third bishop of Cuzco, Sebastián de Lartaún, the report
describes various rituals that were conducted in Cuzco during the
last years of the Inca Empire. Molina was a priest of the Hospital for
the Natives of Our Lady of Succor in Cuzco and he served for nearly
twenty years as the preacher general (*predicador general*) of the city.
Molina was also an outstanding Quechua speaker, and his advanced
language skills allowed him to record both the prayers and the religious celebrations of the Incas in unprecedented detail.

Molina's account was written during a period of growing Spanish domination and accelerated violence against the so-called idolatrous religions of the Andean peoples. Soon after the Spaniards took
control of the imperial city of Cuzco (1534), they began to discour-
age the ritual activities of the Incas. Over the next several decades,
as the Europeans gradually increased their power in the Andes,
they pressured the indigenous peoples to stop practicing their religious activities. Polo de Ondegardo (1916: 31) indicates that only
a few vestiges of the most important Inca celebrations remained in
the city during his first term as chief magistrate (1558–1560), and
many of those were being practiced in secret. By the mid-1570s, indigenous ceremonies had all but disappeared in the former capital.
Within this context of rapidly changing cultural practices, Molina's
Account of the Fables and Rites of the Incas is exceptionally important.

It is based on the testimonies of the older indigenous men of Cuzco who were among the last surviving eyewitnesses of the rituals conducted at the height of Inca rule.

Molina begins his work, after a brief introduction, by recording various Andean myths. These are followed by short discussions of *quipus*, the knotted recording devices of the Incas, and the early life of Pachacuti Inca Yupanqui, the ninth ruler of Cuzco. Information is also provided on the major gods and shrines (*huacas*) of the Incas, as well as on different classes of sorcerers, healers, and fortune-tellers.

He then discusses the major rituals that occurred in Cuzco during each month of the year. These accounts are perhaps the greatest of Molina's contributions, as he offers many details that are not provided by other writers. Most importantly, he provides rich descriptions of the Cuzco solstice celebrations as well as the Citua celebration, during which the city was ritually cleansed, and the annual male initiation ritual. Readers of Molina's work must, however, be careful as they compare his ritual accounts to those offered by other early colonial authors, because all of Molina's ritual descriptions are off by one month. For example, those rituals that are generally thought to have occurred in June, are listed by Molina under the heading of May, and those celebrations that are thought to have occurred in December are listed in his description for November. Once this adjustment is made, comparisons between Molina and other sources can confidently be made.

After describing the ritual calendar, Molina offers shorter descriptions of several Inca rites that were not tied to a specific month (e.g., birth rituals, first hair-cutting celebrations, female initiation rites, and marriages). The manuscript ends with concise descriptions of the Capacocha ritual, in which all the shrines of the empire were offered sacrifices, as well as the Taqui Onqoy movement, a religious cult that spread across the Andes during the late 1560s–early 1570s. Throughout the manuscript, Molina also provides transcriptions of various Quechua prayers.[1]

The manuscript is not dated, and it is not known for certain when the *Account of the Fables and Rites of the Incas* was completed.

Nevertheless, most researchers who have worked with the document believe it was written between 1573 and 1575 (e.g., Romero 1943; Porras Barrenechea 1986; Urbano 2008a, 2008b). Since the text refers to the fall of Vilcabamba and the death of the last Inca, it is certain that the manuscript was written after 1572. However, the earliest date for the document is more precisely set by Lartaún's ascension to the Cuzco bishopric. Lartaún was appointed as the third bishop of Cuzco in 1570, yet he did not arrive in the city until 28 June 1573, and he formally entered the office the following week on 4 July 1573 (Esquivel y Navia 1980: 232, 246; Vasco de Contreras y Valverde 1982: 96). Since Molina indicates in the opening sentence of the *Account of the Fables and Rites of the Incas* that the report was written at the request of Bishop Lartaún, the document must have been composed after early July 1573. The latest date for the manuscript is suggested by a letter written by Francisco de Toledo (1943: xxiii) on 4 November 1575, in which the viceroy notes that Molina had already "busied himself learning and understanding the ancient rites and ceremonies that those Indians had."

AN OVERVIEW OF THE LIFE OF CRISTÓBAL DE MOLINA

The basic known facts of Cristóbal de Molina's life are few, and most have already been reviewed by other authors (Markham 1873; Thayer Ojeda 1920; Loayza 1943; Porras Barrenechea 1986; Urbano and Duviols 1989; Calvo Pérez and Urbano 2008; Urbano 2008a, 2008b, 2008c).[2] From Molina's own statements, we know that he was born in Baeza, Spain, sometime before 1530,[3] but there is no other information concerning his life before he arrived in Cuzco in 1556 at the age of about 27 (see "The Life and Times of Cristóbal de Molina"). Cuzco remained Molina's primary residence until his death on 29 May 1585, although he was called upon during his lifetime to make various trips into the surrounding provinces (Porras Barrenechea 1986: 352; Millones 1990: 224–225).

Perhaps because of his linguistic abilities, Molina was appointed as the priest of the Hospital for the Natives of Our Lady of Succor in Cuzco in 1565 (Porras Barrenechea 1986: 350).[4] The following decade was a time of great social upheaval in the central Andes marked by a resurgence of indigenous ritual practices, against which the Spaniards launched a series of repressive anti–idolatry campaigns. It was also a time of great political change, during which the last independent royal Inca, Tupac Amaru, was captured and killed. During this turbulent era, Molina's responsibilities grew as he became the preacher general of the Cuzco parishes. He was also appointed as an inspector general (*visitador general*) by the ecclesiastical council of Cuzco and asked to visit various territories for evidence of idolatry.[5]

Around 1572 Molina authored a work on the history of the Incas. Although this manuscript is now lost, we know that he gave a copy to Lartaún. Molina's history must have impressed the bishop, as Lartaún then requested that Molina write a second report focusing on the myths and rituals of the Incas. Although Lartaún instituted a series of rigorous reforms in the Cuzco region while he was bishop (Vasco de Contreras y Valverde 1982: 96), Molina won Lartaún's favor and was asked to continue in his positions as priest of the Hospital of the Indians and preacher general of the city.

Like several other Spaniards who conducted interviews in Cuzco during the early Colonial Period (e.g., Ruiz de Navamuel 1882, 1940a, 1940b; Sarmiento de Gamboa 2007), Molina sought out the older indigenous men who had lived in the city during the final years of the Inca Empire. He specifically mentions having interviewed men who participated in state rituals during the lives of the last three indigenous rulers of Cuzco, writing: "To this end, I ordered to assemble a number of very elderly men who witnessed and performed those ceremonies and rituals during [the] time of Huayna Capac, Huascar Inca, and Manco Inca, and some leaders and priests who were of those times." However, unlike most of his contemporaries working in Cuzco, Molina was well qualified to conduct these interviews in Quechua.

One of the most important ecclesiastical events of the early Colonial Period was the Third Lima Provincial Council (1582–1583).

The provincial councils were held periodically to settle issues of church hierarchy and to provide support for the evangelistic activities of the Church (Oré 1982; Timberlake 2008: 97). The third council was especially critical for Lartaún, as some twenty-three charges had been filed against him from different officials in Cuzco (Millones 2008: 21). Since Lartaún died in Lima on 9 October 1583, before the council concluded, many of the charges were never resolved.

Molina also traveled to Lima to attend the council. As he left the Cuzco region, Molina carried a letter, dated 6 June 1582, from the leaders (*caciques principales*) of the eight parishes of the city, who were requesting that Viceroy Martín Enríquez (1581–1583) confer tax-exempt status on them (Porras Barrenechea 1986: 353; Urbano 1990: 276–277). Several of these men are also mentioned in Sarmiento de Gamboa's (2007) *History of the Incas,* and they may have served as informants for both Molina and Sarmiento de Gamboa. Molina's language skills were no doubt welcomed by the council as it toiled with one of its central tasks: the production of three trilingual (Spanish, Quechua, and Aymara) religious works to aid in the teaching of the Christian doctrine. However, while in Lima, Molina became sick and left the city before the council ended, so it is not known how much he actually helped the council with the publications (Millones 1990: 227).

It is also worth noting that Molina testified two times in Cuzco, once before and once after the Third Lima Provincial Council, at inquiries into the services and anti-idolatry campaigns of Cristóbal de Albornoz.[6] The first took place in Cuzco on 14 January 1577 (Millones 1990: 181–182). In his statement, Molina, who is simply introduced as a cleric priest (*clérigo presbítero*), indicated that he had known Albornoz for more than ten years and that Albornoz had successfully completed anti-idolatry campaigns in the area of Arequipa and Huamanga (modern Ayacucho). Molina was called again to give testimony some seven years later, on 28 March 1584, on the services of Albornoz (Millones 1990: 223–228). This time Molina is introduced into the record in far more elaborate terms as "the illustrious Cristóbal de Molina, cleric priest, preacher general of the natives of this city, who was also inspector general of this bishopric." This 1584 testimony is the last substantial document we have on Molina. He died in Cuzco a year and a half later at the approximate age of fifty-six.

THE *HISTORY OF THE INCAS* AND OTHER WORKS BY CRISTÓBAL DE MOLINA

Molina wrote at least two reports on the Incas. Although no copy of Molina's first report, commonly referred to as the *History of the Incas*, has survived, we know that it existed because Molina records giving a copy of it to Bishop Lartaún. This is noted in the opening statement of Molina's *Account of the Fables and Rites of the Incas*, where he also provides a brief summary of his earlier report.

> The account that I gave to Your Most Illustrious Lordship [described] the dealings, origin, lives, and customs of the Incas who were the lords of this land; how many there were, who their wives were, and the laws they made, [the] wars they waged, and [the] people and nations they conquered. Because in some parts of that account I discussed the ceremonies and rituals they established, although not in much detail, I thought it was proper now, principally because Your Most Reverend Lordship has requested it of me, to expend additional effort so that Your Most Reverend Lordship [can] learn about the ceremonies, rituals, and idolatries that these Indians had.

Molina also refers to his first report several times within the text of his *Account on the Fables and Rites of the Incas*. For example, Molina specifically notes that his history contained a retelling of the Pacaritambo origin myth. In this myth, the first Inca, Manco Capac, along with his brothers and sisters, emerged from a cave called Tambotoco in the area of Pacaritambo (Bauer 1991). As they traveled to Cuzco, one of Manco Capac's brothers, Ayarcache, was turned into stone at the summit of Huanacauri, becoming an important shrine of the Cuzco region. Molina refers to the creation of this shrine in the following: "[Huanacauri was] their principal *huaca*, which they said was the brother of Manco Capac, from whom they say they descended. So as to not make [this report] lengthy, I will not discuss the fable of this *huaca* here, having [already] made reference to it in the *History of the Incas* that I have done." Molina also indicates that his telling of the myth appeared near the beginning of his earlier work, writing, "Because this [conversion of Ayarcache into stone] was included and discussed at length in the fable at the beginning of the *History [of the Incas]*, which Your Most Illustrious Majesty has, I do not discuss it here. Your Most Illustrious Lordship can read it there." We also know that Molina's *History of the Incas* contained a description of the life of Inca Yupanqui, since Molina notes, "Throughout his life, as is discussed in the account that Your Lordship has, everything [Inca Yupanqui] conquered and subjected was in the name of the Sun, his father, and of the Creator." Furthermore, within Molina's account of Inca Yupanqui's life there appears to have been a section dedicated to the laws and sayings of this Inca king, since Molina notes the following in his religious report: "Concerning the laws and customs [that] he decreed, I stand by [the information in] the account." Since Inca Yupanqui[7] was among the most important rulers of Cuzco, it is not surprising that his life was described in Molina's *History of the Incas.*[8]

Researchers have long suggested that parts of Molina's *History of the Incas* may be preserved within Miguel Cabello Valboa's *Miscelánea antártica* (1586), as this author notes that he used the work of the "venerable Father Cristóbal de Molina," along with those of several other writers, to research the origins of the Inca kings (Markham 1873: viii–ix; Cabello Valboa 1951: 259–260). Both Cabello Valboa and Molina were in Lima for the Third Lima Provincial Council, and perhaps this is when Cabello Valboa gained access to Molina's manuscript (Núñez-Carvallo 2008: 91).[9]

A copy of Molina's *History of the Incas* must also have been archived somewhere in Cuzco. Dean Vasco de Contreras y Valverde, writing in Cuzco in 1649, specifically mentions it as an important source for his overview on the history of the city:

> They give the same origin of the city's foundation as they attribute to the descent and royal blood of the Incas. I have found another version that mentions it, and in some length, in a manuscript that, by command of Viceroy Don Francisco de Toledo, was written by Father Cristóbal de Molina. [He was an] ancient priest [and] scrutinizer of the intricate *quipu* annals of those times or, better said, labyrinths where the Indians would barbarically imprison the memoirs of their ancient past. (Vasco de Contreras y Valverde 1982: 43 [1649]; my translation)

It is widely assumed, based on the opening line of the *Account of the Fables and Rites of the Incas*, that Molina wrote his *History of the Incas* at the request of Lartaún on the bishop's arrival in Cuzco (Urbano and Duviols 1989; Calvo Pérez and Urbano 2008; Urbano 2008b, 2008c). Yet it should be noted that Molina only indicates that he had *given* a copy of his history to Lartaún and that the bishop had then requested that a second study be made on the rituals of the Incas. Vasco de Contreras y Valverde's reference to Molina's *History of the Incas,* provided above, yields additional information on the social contexts as well as the creation data of the manuscript. He specifically states that Molina's history was written at the request of Viceroy Toledo and that it was based on readings of *quipus* (knotted cords used by the Incas to encode numbers and other information). The request would have been made during Toledo's relatively brief stay in Cuzco (ca. February 1571–October 1572). The request would also have been among several others that Toledo made to various Spaniards, including Sarmiento de Gamboa (2007) and Ruiz de Navamuel (1882, 1940a, 1940b), to research the history of the Incas.

There was a third document that Molina also sent to Bishop Lartaún; however, it is unclear if Molina was the actual author of the manuscript or if he was only passing along information collected by someone else. While describing the shrines (*huacas*) of the

Cuzco region, Molina writes: "There were so many places in Cuzco that were dedicated for sacrifices that it would be very tedious if I describe them here. And because all the ways they sacrificed [at them] are included in the *Account of the Huacas* that I gave to Your Most Illustrious Majesty, I will not include this [information] here." Bernabé Cobo (1990) is known to have copied a large document, now lost, by an unknown writer into his chronicle that included a detailed description of the shrines of the Cuzco region. The above passage by Molina has led some researchers to suggest that Molina may have been the author of this shrine document (Rowe 1946: 300; Zuidema 1964; Porras Barrenechea 1986). John Rowe (1980: 7), however, has pointed out that Molina does not specifically claim authorship of the shrine document but simply states that he gave the bishop a copy. Compelling evidence now suggests that Molina did indeed only *provide* a shrine document to the bishop and that the original author of this document, which Cobo later copied into his work, was Polo de Ondegardo. The shrine document was most likely written around 1559 during Polo de Ondegardo's first term as the chief magistrate of Cuzco (Bauer 1998: 13–22; 1999).

CRISTÓBAL DE ALBORNOZ AND CRISTÓBAL DE MOLINA

Cristóbal de Albornoz was one of the principal leaders in the Church's struggle against the autochthonous religions of the Andes in the immediate postconquest era. From 1568 until his death in the early 1600s, Albornoz led a series of campaigns in the Peruvian highlands to identify and destroy native shrines and to punish the individuals and communities who worshipped them (Millones 2008). He was first assigned the position of inspector general [*visitador general*] in the area of Arequipa (1568) and was then sent on a longer assignment (1569–1571) to Huamanga at the request of the ecclesiastical council of Cuzco and the governor of Peru, Lope García de Castro (Albornoz 1984: 215). It was during this period that a young indigenous man named Felipe Guaman Poma de Ayala, who would later become a writer, came into contact with Albornoz (Figure 1.1).

FIGURE 1.1

Guaman Poma de Ayala (1980 [ca. 1615]: 675 [689]) illustrated Cristóbal de Albornoz and his assistant, Juan Cocha Quispe, during an anti-idolatry campaign against the Taqui Onqoy movement (ca. 1564–1572). The caption reads "First Chapter of Visitor. Cristóbal de Albornoz, visitor general of the Holy Mother Church, good justices, judge." (Courtesy of Det Kongelige Bibliotek.)

In 1570, while still in Huamanga, Albornoz met Viceroy Toledo, who was himself on a general inspection, working his way from Lima to Cuzco (Levillier 1940). Toledo reconfirmed Albornoz's authority and gave him the title of Inspector General [*visitador general*] of Chinchaysuyo (Millones 1990: 179, 181–182; 2008). Albornoz's anti-idolatry campaigns were largely focused on crushing the newly discovered Taqui Onqoy movement (ca. 1564–1572). During his many campaigns, Albornoz was personally responsible for the destruction of thousands of *huacas* and the persecution of a vast number of individuals.[10] His activities in the provinces of Soras, Apcaras, and Lucanas are especially well documented (Millones 1990).

Molina and Albornoz interacted for several decades. Molina first met Albornoz soon after the latter's arrival in Cuzco (1568), and they both spent the rest of their lives in the city, working under various bishops (Millones 2008). They were also both very active in the anti-idolatry movements of their times. For example, while Albornoz was inspecting Arequipa and Huamanga, it seems that Molina was working as an inspector in the Cuzco parishes (Millones 1990: 224). They also held each other in great esteem. Albornoz was especially impressed with Molina's language abilities, and Molina admired Albornoz for the completeness and effectiveness of his inspections. As part of Molina's work for the bishopric of Cuzco, he visited both Arequipa and Huamanga after Albornoz had conducted operations in these regions. As noted above, Molina testified twice (1577 and 1584) on Albornoz's success in destroying local shrines and punishing the local practitioners of idolatry.

Molina and Albornoz were also in close contact while in Cuzco and appear to have worked together on certain occasions. At one such event, Molina preached to a large crowd on the day that two leaders of the Taqui Onqoy movement, who had been brought to Cuzco by Albornoz, were publicly punished (Millones 1990: 181, 225). Molina was also approached by Albornoz with the suggestion that they should join together "to cast a sweeping net so that no sorcery or idolatry would be left without being destroyed" (Millones 1990: 227). They also both attended the Third Lima Provincial Council (1582–1583), although they did not meet in the city but encountered each other somewhere outside of Lima, while Molina was on his journey back to Cuzco and Albornoz was arriving (Millones 1990: 227).

VICEROY FRANCISCO TOLEDO AND CRISTÓBAL DE MOLINA

Francisco de Toledo was appointed to the viceroyalty of Peru (1569–1581) with unprecedented powers to calm growing disorder in the Spanish colony. Soon after arriving in Lima, he set out on an inspection of the Andes that was to last four years. Toledo reached the Cuzco region in late February of 1571 and departed for the Lake Titicaca region more than a year and a half later in October of 1572. During the course of his travels, Toledo collected information concerning the history of the Incas, and this research continued while he was in the imperial heartland. While in Cuzco, Toledo asked Molina to interview various official *quipu* keepers to learn more about the history of the Incas. Similarly, on orders of Toledo, Gabriel de Loarte and Álvaro Ruiz de Navamuel conducted a series of interviews in the Cuzco region on the history of the Incas (Levillier 1940). Finally, Sarmiento de Gamboa (2007), who was then the royal cosmographer traveling with Toledo, researched and wrote a *History of the Incas*, which was publicly read to the leaders of the different kin groups of the city on 29 February and 1 March 1572 before being sent to Spain.

Sarmiento's manuscript is of special interest to this study, since it begins with a retelling of several Andean myths, including Viracocha's creation of the world, Viracocha's activities at Tiahuanaco, and the Cañari origin myth. These same myths are also found in Molina's *Account of the Fables and Rites of the Incas*. Although the two texts contain the same myths, each version gives unique details, making it clear that Molina did not copy Sarmiento's work. Compare, for example, Molina's and Sarmiento de Gamboa's introductions to the Cañari origin myth:

In the province of Quito there is a province called Cañaribanba, and so the Indians who live there are called Cañaris after the
name of the province. They say that at the time of the Flood,
two brothers escaped to a very high hill called Huacayñan that
is in that province. They say in the fable that as the waters were
rising, the hill [also] did; hence the water was not able to reach
them. (Molina)

They say that in the time of the *unu pachacuti* flood there was a
hill called Huasano in a town called Tomebamba in the province of Quito. Today the natives of that land [still] point it out.
Two Cañari men climbed this hill; one of them was named
Ataorupagui and the other Cusicayo. As the waters kept rising,
the mountain swam and floated in such a way that it was never
covered by the floodwaters. Thus the two Cañaris escaped.
(Sarmiento de Gamboa 2007: 46 [1572: Ch. 6])

Although the two narratives are distinct, their similarities do imply
that the authors shared some of the same informants.[11] Since it is
known that both Molina and Sarmiento de Gamboa were asked by
Viceroy Toledo to write histories of the Incas in 1571–1572, and they
both did so by interviewing the oldest surviving indigenous leaders
of Cuzco, it is not surprising that they shared informants, or perhaps
even attended the same interviews.

One of the most important events to occur during Toledo's
time in Cuzco was the capture of Tupac Amaru, the last independent Inca, in the remote region of Vilcabamba. A faction of the Inca
nobility had retreated into the mountains of Vilcabamba in 1537 and
had inspired a long-running guerrilla war against the Spaniards. Toledo ordered a large-scale raid on Vilcabamba in June of 1572 to end
this resistance. During the raid, Tupac Amaru was captured, and he
arrived in chains in Cuzco on 21 September. Three days later, after a
hastily arranged trial, Tupac Amaru was beheaded. During his brief
time in Cuzco, Tupac Amaru was not only being judged but was also
being converted to Christianity. Although a number of leading cler-

gymen questioned the charges brought against Tupac Amaru and begged for mercy, Toledo was relentless in his zeal to kill the Inca and thus fatally weaken the long-standing indigenous resistance to Spanish rule. Antonio de la Calancha (1981: 1883) and Baltazar de Ocampo (1923: 172) both note that Molina was with Tupac Amaru on the day of his execution. Ocampo, having been an actual eyewitness to the event, provides the most detailed description:

> [Tupac Amaru] was accompanied on either side by the two mentioned friars and by Father Alonso de Barzana, of the Company of Jesus, and Father Molina, cleric preacher of the Our Lady of Succor of the Hospital Parish, who went teaching and saying things of great consolation to his soul. They brought him to a scaffold that was built on high in the center of the plaza, beside the cathedral. They led him up there, and those fathers preached to him and conformed his soul with sacred preparations. (Ocampo 1923: 172 [1610]; my translation)

Although Molina was on the scaffold with Tupac Amaru when he was killed, he may not have been one of the religious leaders of Cuzco who had asked for leniency. This is suggested by the fact that in his *Account of the Fables and Rites of the Incas*, Molina not only condemns the Inca's activities in the Vilcabamba region, calling it a den of thieves, but also praises Toledo's defeat of the independent Incas, writing that "Lord Viceroy Don Francisco de Toledo defeated and expelled them from there, through which God Our Lord was greatly served."

Whatever Molina's views toward Tupac Amaru, it is clear that the priest impressed Viceroy Toledo. Some three years later, on 4 November 1575, while Toledo was in Arequipa, the viceroy wrote a letter to the authorities in Cuzco praising Molina's language abilities and his extensive religious work within the Cuzco parishes. In the letter, Toledo (1943: xxiv) orders an adjustment of Molina's annual salary on the condition that he continue to preach to the Indians of all the Cuzco parishes, including "each Sunday, and on all important religious days of the year, in the central plaza beside the city's main church." It is clear that Molina retained this position until close to his death, since in 1584 he is still being introduced as the preacher general of Cuzco. Most significantly for this study, Toledo's letter indicates that Molina had, by 1575, already collected information "on the ancient rites and ceremonies" of the Incas, a clear reference to the materials included in Molina's second report to Bishop Lartaún.

CRISTÓBAL DE MOLINA, LUIS DE OLIVERA,
AND THE TAQUI ONQOY MOVEMENT

In 1564, while serving as a priest in the relatively remote province of Parinacocha, Luis de Olivera noted that previous missionary activities had largely failed and that there was a resurgence—or perhaps simply the strong persistence—of native religious beliefs. On further investigation, he found that a growing social movement was turning indigenous peoples away from the teachings of the Church and encouraging them to return to worshipping local shrines. This movement was active not only in his parish but also in the nearby area of Acarí and various other regions of the Andes, including the largest cities. Olivera attempted to root out this "heresy" in the area of Parinacocha, and he denounced the movement to other Church officials, including the archbishop of Lima and the bishops of Cuzco and Charcas.[12]

In the final pages of his *Account of the Fables and Rites of the Incas*, Molina turns his attention to the events first recorded by Olivera in Parinacocha and later witnessed by other Spaniards across the central Andes. Basing his information on the (now-lost) report written by Olivera, Molina writes the following introduction:

> About ten years ago, more or less, a disaffection began to spread among the Indians of this land, during which they performed a type of song that they called *taqui onqoy*. Because Luis de Olivera, a lay cleric in Parinacocha Province, which is in the

bishopric of Cuzco, was the first to witness this disaffection or idolatry while he was [the] priest of that territory, he explains here about the manner in which they carried it out and why.

The discovery of this sect, now referred to as the Taqui Onqoy (*taqui* = to dance; *onqoy* = to fall ill)[13] movement, provided the impetus for a series of massive campaigns aimed at destroying the indigenous religions of the Andes.[14] Olivera, Molina, and Albornoz were active participants in those campaigns, and their anti-idolatry activities brought them into close contact with each other. For example, after Olivera had returned from the countryside to work in Cuzco, Albornoz conducted an official inspection of Olivera's former Parinacocha parish, where he found that the cult had continued to grow.[15] Later, Albornoz also captured several leaders of the movement, and he brought them to Cuzco to be publicly punished. At the time, Olivera was working as the secretary of the ecclesiastical council of Cuzco, and he heard the sermon that Molina, as preacher general of the city, delivered to the natives on the day that the indigenous leaders were punished. Following this event, Molina visited the Ayacucho region to confirm that the heresy had been extinguished (Millones 1990: 176–182). Later still, in 1577, Olivera and Molina provided sequential testimonies in support of Albornoz's many years of work for the Church.[16]

The Taqui Onqoy movement was spread by native men and women who believed that they had become possessed by local deities. These "preachers" visited various communities proclaiming that the time of the *huacas* was at hand. They suggested that although the gods of the Andes had been defeated with the arrival of Pizarro, the *huacas* were rising again and would soon defeat the Spaniards, at which time control of the Andean world would be returned to its indigenous people. Molina writes the following:

> . . . they believed that all the *huacas* of the kingdom that the
> Christians had demolished and burned had come back to life,
> and had formed themselves into two sides: some had joined

with the *huaca* of Pachacama[c] and the others with the *huaca* Titica[ca]. [They said] that all of them were flying around in the air, ordering [the people] to give battle to God and defeat Him. [And] they [claimed] that they were already defeating Him. And that when the Marquis [i.e., Pizarro] entered this land, God had defeated the *huacas,* and the Spaniards [had defeated] the Indians. But now, the world had turned around, [so] God and the Spaniards would be defeated this time, and all the Spaniards [would] die, their cities would be flooded, and the sea would rise and drown them so that no memory would be left of them.

This reversal of fortune was to come about through the supernatural intervention of the local shrines, and those natives who wanted to be saved from the coming apocalypse needed to renege their Catholic faith and reject all things Spanish. They also needed to return to their native religious teachings and worship the traditional *huacas* of the Andes. In short, it was believed that with the rise of the autochthonous gods, the period of Spanish rule over the Andes was coming to an end. Molina, using information provided by Olivera, provides a summary of the movement:

> Within this apostasy, they believed that God, Our Lord, had made the Spaniards, Castile, and the animals and supplies of Castile, but that the *huacas* had made the Indians, this land, and the supplies that the Indians had before [the arrival of the Spaniards]. . . . They went about preaching this resurrection of the *huacas,* saying that the *huacas* now were flying through the air, dried out and dying of hunger, because the Indians no longer made sacrifices nor poured *chicha* to them. [The Indians said] that they had planted many *chacras* with worms to sow them in the hearts of the Spaniards, [in the] livestock of Castile and [in the] horses, and also in the hearts of the Indians who remained Christians. [They said] that [the *huacas*] were angry with all of the [Christian Indians] because they had been baptized and that [the *huacas*] would kill them all if they did

not return to them, reneging on the Catholic faith. Those who wanted the friendship and grace [of the *huacas*] would live in prosperity, grace, and health. In order to return to [the *huacas*], they were to fast some days, not eat salt or chili, nor have sexual relations, nor eat colored maize, nor eat things of Castile, nor use them in food or in clothing, nor enter the churches, nor pray, nor respond to the calls of the priests, nor call themselves by Christian names. [They said] that in this way, they would return to the love of the *huacas* and they would not be killed. They also [preached] that the time of the Incas was returning and that the *huacas* [were] no longer entering stones, clouds, or springs to speak, but [they were] now themselves entering the Indians and making them speak.

The Taqui Onqoy gained its name through the trancelike state that members of this movement experienced. Once possessed, individuals would speak on behalf of the *huacas* and instruct the villagers on how they should react to the coming cataclysm.

The Spaniards were both surprised by the development of this movement and mystified by the peculiar form in which it was manifested. Molina and others linked the Taqui Onqoy movement with the independent Incas entrenched in the Vilcabamba region.[17] Although the continued resistance to Spanish rule by Manco Inca and his sons may have served as an inspiration to many natives, it was not the source of the Taqui Onqoy movement. Instead, it appears that the movement drew its origins from the nearly incomprehensible loss of control and the dramatic cultural transformations that were occurring across the Andes. Within just a few decades, the peoples of the Andes had seen the collapse of the Inca Empire, the decimation of their populations by unknown diseases, and their practical enslavement by strangers who looked and acted unlike any humans they had ever seen before.

Although Lope García de Castro, who was then interim governor of Peru (1564–1569), as well as church officials such as Molina, Olivera, and Albornoz, may have been puzzled by the appearance of the Taqui Onqoy movement and its profoundly religious dimensions, modern scholars are not. It is now widely accepted that the Taqui Onqoy movement falls within a broad class of social actions frequently termed "millenarian movements" (Millones 1964; Ossio 1973; Wachtel 1977; Stern 1982a, 1982b; MacCormack 1991; Mumford 1998).[18] These movements represent innovative religious responses that offer hope to disadvantaged portions of a population. Numerous millenarian movements have been recorded throughout history, and they frequently occur in the wake of colonialism, such as the North American Ghost Dance of the 1890s and the South Pacific Cargo Cults of the 1940s. These movements tend to call for a return to traditional customs and a rejection of the newly dominant social order. They also include predictions that the current social conditions will be overturned by supernatural forces. Most of these movements are peaceful, but colonial powers often see them as a threat to their control over the civil population and go to great efforts to extinguish them.

Indigenous resistance against the culture and power of Spain was widespread and took many forms over the next century, yet the specific Taqui Onqoy movement of the central Andes was relatively short-lived. It was first noted by Olivera around 1564, and Molina reports that it lasted about seven years. The end of the movement, ca. 1571, coincides with Albornoz's prolonged anti-idolatry activities in the Ayacucho region, where he is credited with "pulling the movement out by its roots" (Millones 1990: 64) and punishing several of its leaders in Cuzco.

As Molina introduces the Taqui Onqoy movement, he also provides information about what appears to have been another set of native beliefs. He suggests that some of the natives of Peru had come to fear contact with the Spaniards, thinking that they were able to extract a curative "ointment" from the indigenous people. Molina writes:

[In] the year of [15]70, and not before, the Indians held and believed that [people] had been sent from Spain to this kingdom [to search] for an ointment of the Indians to cure a certain illness for which no medicine was known except for that ointment. In those times [and] for this reason, the Indians went about very secretively, and [they] distanced themselves from the Spaniards to such a degree that no [Indian] wanted to take firewood, herb[s], or other things to a Spaniard's house. They say that [in this way, the Indian] would not be killed inside by having the ointment extracted from him.

This fear is not specifically mentioned in any other colonial account, yet it appears to have developed from the same dismal social conditions that fostered widespread beliefs in the Taqui Onqoy millenarian movement (Wachtel 1977). In the above passage, Molina documents that certain indigenous people believed that an ointment, most certainly fat, was being extracted by the Spaniards to cure a European disease.[19] By the 1570s, an enormous number of native people had died as a result of the European infectious diseases (including smallpox, typhus, measles, and influenza) that had swept through the Andes after contact (Cook 1981, 1998). Native-born people were far more likely to die in these catastrophic epidemics, since they had no natural resistance to the newly introduced microbes. The belief in the ointment-taking abilities of the Spaniards appears to be an indigenous explanation for the prevalent, and disproportional, death of native peoples after the arrival of European diseases. Within this context, the Europeans seemed to have had the ability to extract health from the native populations to save themselves. The belief was factually incorrect, but it provides a powerful metaphor for the social conditions that existed throughout the Colonial Period.

BERNABÉ COBO AND CRISTÓBAL DE MOLINA

In 1653, the Jesuit priest Bernabé Cobo completed his great work *Historia del Nuevo Mundo* (History of the New World), which included an overview of the history of the Incas and a summary of their myths and rituals. Cobo extracted much of his information on the history and religious practices of the Incas from earlier documents stored in different secular and ecclesiastical archives across Peru, but like most writers of his time, he was inconsistent in acknowledging his sources. Furthermore, in some sections he interwove passages from different sources, and in other places he reproduced entire blocks of information (Rowe 1980: 2). Nevertheless, it is clear that Cobo had a copy of Molina's *Account of the Fables and Rites of the Incas* and that he relied on it heavily. Molina's manuscript is specifically mentioned in the *History of the New World*, as Cobo discusses the major sources he used to research the Incas. After discussing Polo de Ondegardo's famed 1559 document outlining the history of the Incas, as well as a second, lesser-known work that was produced during Viceroy Toledo's stay in Cuzco, Cobo describes Molina's work:

> And a little later, another general meeting of all the old Indians that had lived during the reign of the Inca Guayna Capac was held in the city of Cuzco itself by Cristobal de Molina, a parish priest at the hospital of the natives in the Parish of Nuestra Señora de los Remedios; this meeting was ordered by Bishop Sebastian de Lartaun and confirmed the same things as the previous meetings; the result was a copious account of the rites and fables that the Peruvian Indians practiced in pagan times. This information is substantially the same as that of Licentiate Polo and that of the report that was made by order of Francisco de Toledo. Both Toledo's report and the account by Molina have come into my possession. (Cobo 1979: 100 [1653: Bk. 12, Ch. 2])

Cobo reproduced many large blocks of text directly from Molina and lightly paraphrased others.[20] We have marked the major sections of Molina that were copied by Cobo in the footnotes of our English translation.

SUMMARY

The *Account of the Fables and Rites of the Incas* remains an invaluable source of information about the Incas of Peru. Molina's facility with Quechua and prolonged contact with the Andean people made him uniquely suited to provide an in-depth report on precontact Andean culture. Having arrived in Cuzco during a critical period of cultural transformations, Molina took detailed notes about how rituals had been conducted in the imperial capital during the final years of the empire. His report on the religious activities of the Incas offers levels of detail and cultural insights that are rarely matched by other early colonial writers. Molina's record of Inca rituals is all the more important, since his first work, on the history of the Incas, has been lost to antiquity.

This present work provides a new English translation of Molina's report on Inca myths and rituals. The only other English translation was completed by Markham in 1873. Since that time, a vast amount of new information, both historical and archaeological, has become available and standards of translation have changed. We hope that this work will offer new insights into the religious activities of the Incas and will aid others to explore and understand the Andean past.

Account of the Fables and Rites of the Incas

WRITTEN BY CRISTÓBAL DE MOLINA

Priest of the parish of Our Lady of Succor of the Hospital for the Natives of the city of Cuzco, addressed to the Most Reverend Lord Bishop Don Sebastián de Lartaún of His Majesty's Council.

Chapter 1

INTRODUCTION

The account that I gave to Your Most Illustrious Lordship[1] [described] the dealings, origin, lives, and customs of the Incas who were the lords of this land; how many there were, who their wives were, and the laws they made, [the] wars they waged, and [the] people and nations they conquered.[2] Because in some parts of that account I discussed the ceremonies and rituals they established, although not in much detail, I thought it was proper now, principally because Your Most Reverend Lordship has requested it of me, to expend additional effort so that Your Most Reverend Lordship [can] learn about the ceremonies, rituals, and idolatries that these Indians had. To this end, I ordered to assemble a number of very elderly men who witnessed and performed those ceremonies and rituals during [the] time of Huayna Capac, Huascar Inca, and Manco Inca,[3] and some leaders and priests who were of those times.

Chapter 2

ORIGIN MYTHS

*T*o understand the origins of their idolatries, because it is true that these [Incas] did not use writing, they had in a House of the Sun called Poquen Cancha,[1] which is next to Cuzco, the life of each of the Incas, the lands that [each of them] conquered, and their origin [myths] painted with figures on boards.[2] Among those images they had the following fable.

It was during the life of Manco Capac, who was the first Inca, that they began to claim and call themselves "children of the Sun" and when the Sun worship and idolatry started. [During this time,] they heard important news about the Flood. They say that all the [different] people and everything that had been created perished during it. So [it happened that] the waters rose over the highest hills that existed in the world, and hence nothing survived except a man and a woman, who remained in a drum box. [They say] that when the waters subsided, the wind blew them to Tiahuanaco, which may be more than seventy leagues, more or less, from Cuzco, and that the Creator of All Things ordered them to stay there as *mitimas* [colonists]. There in Tiahuanaco, the Creator began to make the people and nations that are in this land. He made each nation out of clay [and] painted on them the costumes and clothes that each one was to have. And those that were to have [long] hair [he made] with [long] hair, and those that were to have short [hair he made with] short hair. When he finished, he gave each nation the language they were to speak, the songs they were to sing, and the seeds and foods they were to sow.[3]

Once he finished painting and making those nations and clay figures, he gave each and every one life and a soul, to the men as well as to the women. He ordered each and every nation to descend into the earth and afterward to emerge in the parts and places where he would order. Thus, they say that some emerged from caves, others from hills, others from springs, others from lakes, others from the trunks of trees, and other absurdities of this sort. Because they emerged and began to multiply from those places, and since their lineage had begun there, they made those places *huacas* [sacred places or objects] and shrines, in memory of the first of their lineage who had emerged from there. Hence, each nation dresses and wears the costume with which they used to dress their *huaca*. They say that the first [ancestor] to be born at that place was turned into stone there, and others into hawks, condors, and other birds and animals. Therefore, the *huacas* that they worship and use are of different shapes.

There are other nations that say that during the Flood [most of] the people died because of the water, except those who could escape to some hills, caves, and trees, and these were very few. From these [survivors] they began to multiply. Because they escaped [to] and came from those places, they placed stone idols at them in memory of the first [ancestor] who emerged there. They gave each *huaca* the name of the person who they believed had [emerged] from that place. Thus they worshipped them and offered sacrifices of the things that each nation used. Nevertheless, there were some nations that knew, before the Incas conquered them, that there was a Creator of All Things. Although they made some sacrifices to him, they were neither in such amounts nor with such veneration as [those made] to their *huacas*.

Continuing the above fable, they say that during those times the Creator was in Tiahuanaco. They say that because it was his principal seat, there were some magnificent buildings worthy of great admiration there, in which were painted many of the costumes of these Indians, and [there were] many stone statues of men and women. They say that the Creator had turned them into stone because they did not obey his orders (Figures 2.1 and 2.2).[4]

They say that it was night and that he made the Sun, Moon, and Stars there [i.e., at Tiahuanaco]. And that he ordered the Sun, Moon, and Stars to go to the Island of Titicaca, which is nearby, and that from there they should rise to the heavens (Figure 2.3).[5] And as the Sun was rising in [the] shape of a very resplendent man, he called to the Incas and to Manco Capac, [recognizing him] as their leader, and said to him, "You and your descendants will be lords and you will subjugate many nations. Look upon me as [your] father and claim yourselves as my children, and thus you will worship me as your father." Having said this to Manco Capac, he gave him as insignias and weapons the *sumtur paucar* [royal banner][6] and the *champi* [axe] and [the] other insignias that they used, which are like scepters. They had all of these as insignias and weapons. At this point he ordered the Sun, Moon, and Stars to rise to the heavens [and] fix themselves in their places. And thus, they ascended and so placed themselves. Then, at that very instant, Manco Capac and his brothers and sisters, by order of the Creator, descended into

FIGURE 2.1

Tiahuanaco was a sacred place for the Incas, filled with ancient remains. (Photograph by Max T. Vargas, ca. 1930, private collection.)

FIGURE 2.2

The statues of Tiahuanaco were thought to be individuals who had been transformed into stone by the Creator god. (Max T. Vargas, ca. 1930, © President and Fellows of Harvard College, Peabody Museum of Archaeology and Ethnology, 2004.1.433.1.)

the earth and they emerged from the cave of Pacaritambo, from where they claimed to originate, although they say that other nations [also] emerged from that cave.[7] They emerged at dawn, on the first day after the Creator had divided the night from the day. Hence from then onward they retained the surname "Children of the Sun" to call themselves, and worshipped and revered the [Sun] as [their] father.

They also have another fable in which they say that the Creator had two sons, one called Ymaymana Viracocha and the other Tocapo Viracocha. And the Creator, having finished the people and nations; given them clothes and languages; and having sent the Sun,

FIGURE 2.3

The sun was believed by the Incas to have emerged from this outcrop on the Island of the Sun in Lake Titicaca. (Anonymous photograph, ca. 1920, private collection.)

Moon, and Stars from Tiahuanaco, each to their place, as was described; the Creator, who in the language of these Indians is called Pachayachachi and by another name Titiuiracochan,[8] which means "incomprehensible god," went by the road of the sierra inspecting and visiting all the nations to see how they had begun to multiply and to do what he had ordered them to do. He found that some nations had rebelled and had not followed his orders, [so] he turned most of them into stones, in the shape of men and women, with the same clothing that they had worn. The transformation into stones occurred in the following places: in Tiahuanaco, Pucara, and Jauja, where they say he turned the *huaca* called Huarivilca[9] into stone;[10] [as well as] in Pachacama[c], Cajamarca, and other locations. At present there are some large stone statues in those places, and in some areas the statues are almost [as large] as giants, which must have been made by the hands of men during very ancient times. Because the [natives] lack writing and the memory [of these events], they accept this fable by saying that [the people] were turned into stones at the command of the Creator, since they did not follow his orders (Figure 2.4). In Pucara, which is forty leagues from the city

FIGURE 2.4

The Incas built a large temple in the town of Racchi in honor of their Creator god. (Anonymous photograph, ca. 1920–1930, copyright © President and Fellows of Harvard College, Peabody Museum of Archaeology and Ethnology, 2004.29.9845.)

of Cuzco by the Collao road, they say that fire came down from the heavens [on his orders] and burned most of them, and that those who tried to escape were transformed into stones.[11]

The Creator, who they say was the father of Ymaimana Uiracochan and Tocapo Viracochan,[12] ordered that the eldest of his sons, called Ymaymana Viracochan, [which means] "in whose power and hands all things are found," should leave by the road of the Andes and [visit the] forested slopes[13] of all the land. He was to give and assign names to all the trees, large and small, and to the flowers and fruits that they produced, teaching the people which ones were to eat and which were not, and which were good for medicine. Likewise he gave names to all the herbs and flowers and [determined] the season during which they produced their fruits and flowers. He taught [all] this to the people, [including] the herbs that had healing properties and those that could kill.

[The Creator] ordered the other son, named Tocapo Viracochan, which means in their language "Creator in whom all things are included," to travel via the road of the plains, visiting the people and giving names to the rivers and trees that were there; and presenting fruits and flowers to them in the described manner. [The Creator also ordered his sons] to go down to the lowermost [area] of this land, and hence, in doing so, they descended to the sea[shore] at the lowermost [part] of the land. From there they ascended to the heavens after having completed what was [required] on land.

They also say in this same fable that in Tiahuanaco, where they say he made all the people, [the Creator also] made all the different kinds of birds, a male and female of each one, and he gave them [the] songs that each one was to sing. [He ordered] those that were to live in the forested slopes to go there, and those [that were to live] on the land [to go there]. Each one [was sent] to the part and place where they were to live. In this same manner, he made all the different kinds of animals, a male and female of each, and all the different kinds of snakes and other creatures that exist in this land. He ordered each one of those that were to go to the forested slopes to go there and the others to go across the land. He taught the people there all the names and properties that the birds, animals, and other creatures have.

These Indians also held as very true and certain that [neither] the Creator nor his sons were born of woman and that they were immutable, [and] that they were also eternal. Some nations of this land also tell many other absurdities and fables concerning their origins, such that if we were to relate them all, besides being lengthy, they would never end. I will, therefore, provide [only] a few so that you can understand the foolishness and blindness in which they lived.

THE ORIGIN MYTH OF THE CAÑARI

In the province of Quito[14] there is a province called Cañaribanba, and so the Indians who live there are called Cañaris[15] after the name of the province.[16] They say that at the time of the Flood, two brothers escaped to a very high hill called Huacayñan that is in that province. They say in the fable that as the waters were rising, the hill [also] did; hence the water was not able to reach them.[17] After the Flood subsided and they had finished the food that they stored there, they roamed the hills and valleys searching for food. They built a very small house to live in and they sustained themselves on roots and herbs, experiencing many difficulties and hunger. One day, after having gone out to search for food, they returned to their little house and found food prepared and *chicha* [maize beer] to drink, not knowing how it had arrived or who had made it. This continued for about ten days, at the end of which they both decided to try to learn who was helping them so much in a time of great need. Thus the eldest of them decided to hide, and he saw two birds arrive, which they call *aguaque;* they [also] use the alternative name of *torito* and in our language we call them *guacamayos* [macaws]. They came dressed like Cañaris, [with] the hair on their heads tied in front like they do now. When the eldest of them reached the hut, the hidden Indian saw her remove her *lliclla* [mantle], which is the mantle that they use, and she began to prepare food from what they had brought. When he saw that they were very beautiful and that they had faces like women, he came out from hiding and ran toward them. When they saw the Indian, they left with great anger and flew away, without making or leaving that day's food. When the younger brother, who had gone to search for food, returned from the field, he found nothing prepared, unlike the other days. He asked his brother why this was so, and he told him the reason, and they had a great fight over this. Thus the younger brother decided to hide until he [could] see if they [would] return.

After three days, [the] two *huacamayas* [macaws] returned, and they began to prepare food. As [the younger brother] saw this was an opportune time to capture them, he entered after seeing they had prepared food. He ran to the door, closed it, and trapped them inside, [causing] them to become very angry. Then he grabbed the younger one and while he was holding the younger one, the elder [bird] escaped. They say that he joined and had carnal relations with the younger, with whom, over time, he had six sons and daughters. They lived for a long time on that hill, sustaining themselves on the seeds that they planted, which they say the *huacamayas* [macaws] brought. They say that all the Cañaris descend [from] these brothers and sisters, the children of this *huacamaya*, who spread across the province of Cañaribamba. Thus they hold the hill called Huacayñan as a *huaca* and they [hold] the *huacamayas* in great veneration. Their feathers are also greatly valued for their festivities.[18]

THE ORIGIN MYTH OF ANCASMARCA

In the province of the Indians of Ancasmarca,[19] which is five leagues from Cuzco, in the province of Antisuyo, they have the following fable.[20] They say that a month before the Flood arrived,[21] the rams[22] they owned showed great sadness.[23] During the day they did not eat, and at night they were watching the stars to such a degree that the shepherd who took care of them asked them what was happening. To which they [answered by] asking him to look at a group of stars that were assembled [and] there they agreed that the world was to be destroyed by water.[24] Thus, having heard this, the shepherd discussed it with his six sons and daughters, and they decided to gather as much food and livestock as they could, and [then] they climbed a very high hill called Ancasmarca. They say that as the waters rose and covered the earth, the hill grew in such a way that the [waters] never covered it. Afterward, as the waters subsided, the hill also grew smaller. Thus, from the shepherd's six children who escaped [from] there, the province of these Cuyos was repopulated.

Chapter 3

OF *QUIPUS* AND INCA YUPANQUI

hey tell and relate other similar absurdities about the past that, as I have said, I have not included for the sake of brevity. The reason for all this, besides the main fact that they did not know God and they gave themselves over to vices and idolatries, is [that] they were not people who use writing. Because if they [had] used [writing], they would not have [had] such blind and obtuse and foolish errors and fables.

Nevertheless, they used a very clever method of counting with strands of wool with two knots, using different-colored wool in the knots, which they call *quipus* [knotted strings]. They communicated and [still] communicate so well by means of this, [that] they can recall everything that has occurred in this land over the span of five hundred years. They had Indian specialists and masters in these *quipus* and accounts. They transmitted what had passed from generation to generation, embedding it into the memory of the next generation, who miraculously did not forget even the smallest detail that they kept on those *quipus*. These look almost like the strings with which women pray in our Spain,[1] except that they are hanging strands. They kept account [on the *quipus*] of the years, months, and moons to such a degree that no error was committed in a moon, year, or month. However, the [use of *quipus*] was not so [well] organized until after Inca Yupanqui began to rule and conquer this land, since before his time the Incas had not expanded beyond the surroundings of Cuzco, as is told in the account that Your Most Reverend Lordship has.[2] It seems this Inca was the first who began to take account of and to calculate everything, and the one who removed [some] rituals and added [other] rituals and ceremonies. He was also the one who established the twelve months of the year, gave names to each one, and created the ceremonies they hold in each one of them. Even though before the rule [of the Incas], their ancestors did [track the] months and years on their *quipus*, they were not as well organized as when he was Lord, since they were only regulated by the winters and the summers.

This [Lord] was so wise that he started pondering upon the respect and reverence that his ancestors have had for the Sun, noting that they worshipped him as a god who never stopped or rested and who traveled every day around the world. This [Lord] spoke and discussed with those of his council that it was not possible for the Sun to be the god who created everything, because if he were, a small cloud would not be able to pass in front of him and obscure his resplendence so he could not shine. And that if he were the Creator of All Things, then one day he would rest; and from that place he would illuminate the entire world and order what he wanted. This being the case, it was not possible [that the Sun was the Creator], hence there had to be another [god] who ordered and governed him; this was the Pachayachachi, which means "Creator."[3]

Thus, with this agreement and understanding, he ordered the houses and temple of Quis[h]uarcancha[4] built, which is above the houses of Diego Ortiz de Guzmán, going toward the Cuzco plaza, where Hernán López de Segovia now lives (Map 3.1).[5] There he placed the gold statue of the Creator, [which was] the size of a ten-year-old boy.[6] It was shaped like a standing man, his right arm raised high, with the hand almost closed, and the thumb and second finger raised, like a person who was ordering. Although the Incas had knowledge of a Creator of All Things from the beginning, and they revered him and made sacrifices to him, he had not been revered as much as he was from this Inca onward. Thus [Inca Yupanqui] ordered a temple built to him in the capitals of all the provinces that he conquered and to have livestock, servants, *chacras* [fields], and estates [dedicated] to him, from which the sacrifices would be made.

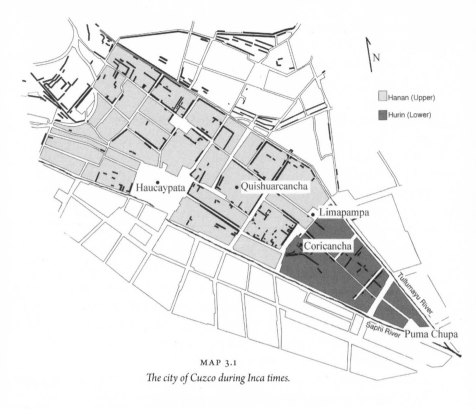

MAP 3.1
The city of Cuzco during Inca times.

This was the Inca who sumptuously built the House of the Sun in Cuzco, because before him, it was very poor and small. The reason [for this] was the following fable. They say that before [Inca Yupanqui] was Lord, he went to visit his father, Viracocha Inca, who was in ~~Çaquajaguxa~~ Sacsahuana,[7] five leagues from Cuzco. As he arrived at a spring called Susurpuquio,[8] he saw a crystal tablet fall into that same spring. Within [the crystal] he saw a figure of an Indian in the following form: three very splendid rays, all of them like the rays of the Sun, radiated upward from the back of his head. Around his shoulders were coiled snakes, [and he wore] on his head a *llayto* [headband] like an Inca. His ears [were] pierced, and he wore ear spools like an Inca. His costume and clothes were also of an Inca. From between his legs appeared the head of a lion,[9] and on his back [was] another lion, the front legs of which seemed to embrace both [of the man's] shoulders. [There was also] a kind of snake that was attached near the top of his back and continued downward.

When he saw that form and figure, Inca Yupanqui started to flee, but from within the spring the form of the statue called him by his name, telling him: "Come here, son, do not be frightened; because I am the Sun, your father, and I know that you will conquer many nations. Take very great care to worship me and remember me in your sacrifices." And with this, the form vanished, but the crystal mirror remained in the spring. The Inca took it and kept it. They say [that] afterward he could see anything that he wanted in it.

With regard to this, once [Inca Yupanqui] was Lord and was able to, he ordered a statue in the form of the Sun, which looked precisely like the one that he had seen in the mirror. He [also] ordered that in the capitals of the provinces of all the lands that he conquered grand temples should be built for [the Sun and] endowed with large estates. He [also] ordered all the people that he conquered to worship and revere him together with the Creator. Throughout his life, as is discussed in the account that Your Lordship has,[10] everything he conquered and subjected was in the name of the Sun, his father, and of the Creator. He said that everything was for them.

It was this Inca who ordered all the nations that he conquered to hold their *huacas* in great veneration and to go to them with their sacrifices, telling [the *huacas*] not to be angry with them for not remembering to revere and worship them [in the past]. He also had houses built for the Thunder.[11] He had a gold statue made [in the] shape of a man and ordered it placed in the temple that he built for him in the city of Cuzco. This *huaca*, together with those of the Sun and the Creator, had its own temple, estates, livestock, and servants for its sacrifices in all of the provinces. Concerning the laws and customs [that] he decreed, I stand by [the information in] the account.[12] So my aim here is to only discuss what is related to the rituals and ceremonies [of the Incas]. He also had in some nations many *huacas* and temples where the devil would give his answers, [such] as in the shrine of Huanacauri[13] in the city of Cuzco.

Chapter 4

THE SORCERERS

*T*hey had many kinds of sorcerers in the provinces,[1] the names and occupations of which were different from one another.[2] The names and occupations are the following:

Calpariçu, which means "those who are able to see the fortune and success of the things that they are asked." For this purpose they would kill birds, lambs, and rams. Inflating the lungs through a certain vein, they would look for certain signs in them by which they could predict what was to happen.[3]

There were others that they called *uirapiricoc* [fat reader], who would burn coca and ram's fat in a fire.[4] They would tell see what was to happen [in the future] through the fluids and signs that were produced during the burning, and they would tell it to those who hired asked them.[5] These were the least believed because they always lied.[6]

There were others called *achicoc* [a type of diviner] who were the fortune-tellers who cast lots with maize and ram dung.[7] They would give their answers depending on whether these resulted in evens or odds, telling those who asked them what they wanted to know.

There were others called *camascas* [shamans] who would tell [others] that the grace and virtue that they possessed had been given by the Thunder.[8] They say that when someone was frightened by a lightning strike, on regaining consciousness, he would claim that the Thunder had given him the skill of either healing with herbs or of answering questions that they were asked. In the same way, when someone survived from some river or great danger, they would say that the devil had appeared before them. And to those whom [he] wanted to heal with herbs, the devil would teach them. Therefore, because of this, there are many great Indian herbalists. He would show other people poisonous herbs to [be used to] kill to kill, and these were [all] called *camascas*.

There were others called *yacarcaes* [types of diviners], and these were natives of Huaro.[9] It seems that because of the occupation they had, these people held great pacts with the devil.[10] [The divinations] were carried out in the following way: they would take some pipes—the upper half were copper and the lower half were silver—the length of an ordinary-size harquebus, as well as some braziers, in which they would light a fire using charcoal.[11] This [charcoal] was blown and lit with those pipes. The demons would give their answers in the fire, saying that it was the soul of the man or woman about whom they were asking, whether they were in Quito or in any other part of those conquered by the Inca. The principal questions they asked were: Who was against the Sun their father? or, Who sought to rebel against the Inca? or, Who in that area was a thief, a murderer, or an adulterer? or, Who lived badly? Thus, through the work of the devil, with this invocation the Inca knew everything that happened in his land. These *yacarcaes* were greatly feared by both the Incas and other people. Wherever he went, he took them with him.

There were also other sorcerers who were in charge of the *huacas*, among whom were some who would intercede between some of the [*huacas*] and the devil.[12] [The sorcerers] would receive their answers and tell either the townspeople what they wanted to know or the individual person who requested [their service]. However, they very rarely gave truthful answers.

According to what they say, all the people of this land used to give confession to the sorcerers who were in charge of the *huacas*. This confession was made [in] public, and to learn if they had confessed [the] truth, the sorcerer would cast lots. In them, by work of the devil, he would see who had confessed a lie, in which case great punishments were given. Since some people had some grave sins punishable by death, they would bribe the sorcerer and confess to him in secret.[13] The Incas and the people of Cuzco always made their confessions in secret, and for the most part, they confessed to the Indians of Huaro, [who were] sorcerers that they used specifically for this purpose. In their confessions, they would accuse themselves of not having revered the Sun, the Moon, and the *huacas*, and of not having kept or celebrated wholeheartedly the festivities of the *raymis*, which are the [celebrations] of the months of the year. They would accuse each other of fornication, [only] because it was against the commandment of the Inca to take another [man's] woman, or to corrupt any maiden, or to take her [as a wife] without the consent of the Inca; not because they held fornication by itself as a sin, since they lacked this understanding.[14] They would [also] accuse each other of murder and theft, holding these as grave sins; the same for gossip, especially if it had been against the Inca or against the Sun.

In the same way, Most Reverend Lord, they would confess that the Creator made the people and everything [else] that existed before the Flood. However, they do not know in what order or how, except for what has been said about Tiahuanaco.

This is what I have been able to learn and obtain regarding their fables, rituals, and origins from all the elders with whom I have dealt and discussed this business.

Chapter 5

THE RITUALS OF THE MONTHS
OF THE YEAR

*T*he types of rituals and sacrifices that they carried out, in each month of the year, are as follows.

MAY

They began recording the year halfway through May,[1] more or less, on the first day of the [new] moon.[2] They called the first month of the year Haucay Llusqui, in which they held the following ceremonies called ~~Intizipaimi~~ Intip Raymi, which means "Celebration of the Sun" (Figure 5.1).[3] In this month they would sacrifice a great quantity of rams of all colors to the Sun. [They would sacrifice] certain [rams] called *huacarpaña* [white alpaca?] that were white and woolly; other rams called *huanacos*; other white [and] woolly *pacos* [alpacas][4] called *cuyllos* [bright whites]; other *pacos* called *paucarpaco[s]* [red alpacas] [that] were red and woolly females; other *pacos* called *oquipaco[s]* [gray alpacas]; other large rams called *chumpi* [chestnut brown] whose color was almost chestnut brown; and other rams called *llanca llama* [black llama], which were black and woolly. They would also sacrifice at this time lambs of the same colors [as the rams]. They performed this sacrifice in the following way:

They went to the Coricancha in the morning, at noon, and at night, bringing the rams that were to be sacrificed that day. They led them around the idols and *huacas*, called Punchao Inca, which was the Sun; the Pachayachachi, which means "Creator" in their words,

FIGURE 5.1

The Inti Raymi celebration as shown by Guaman Poma de Ayala (1980 [1615]: 246 [248]). The caption reads "June, rest from the harvest." Near the bottom of the page is written "[The Inca] drinks with the Sun during the festival of the Sun." (Courtesy of Det Kongelige Bibliotek.)

[which] was another idol [in the] shape of a man; and another idol called Chuqui Ylla Yllapa,[5] which was the *huaca* of lightning, thunder, and lightning bolts. This *huaca* was shaped [like] a person, although its face could not be seen. It also had a gold *llayto* [head band], gold earplugs, and a gold medallion, which they call *canipo*,[6] and it had its clothes folded next to it.

Those *huacas* were placed on a bench, and [while] the live rams went around them,[7] the priests said:

> O Creator, Sun, and Thunder, be forever young and never age.
> [Let] all things be in peace, the people multiply, and food be
> [plentiful]. [Let] everything else always increase.[8]

They said these prayers to the Creator, and they asked the Sun to be forever young and to rise up, giving light and splendor. They did not recognize him as the Creator but as [being] created by the Creator. And they asked the Thunder and Lightning to make rain so there would be food, also knowing that [through] thunder and lightning it would rain by order of the Creator.

In the morning they would send a sheep to Huanacauri, which is the principal *huaca* they have, as mentioned in the *History of the Incas*.[9] There the *tarpuntaes* [priests of the Sun],[10] who were the ones in charge of feeding the *huacas*, would kill and burn it. While they burned it, at the morning sunrise, many Incas and *caciques* [local lords] would go there. [But] before it was burned, they would pull wool off the ram [and would walk] around the sacrifice with the wool in their hands saying:

> O Creator, Sun, and Thunder, may you always be young, may
> the people multiply and always be in peace.

At noon they would burn, in the same way, another ram in the Coricancha, in the courtyard of the aforementioned House of the Sun, which is now the cloister of the friars of the Lord Santo Domingo (Figure 5.2). And at sunset, they would take another [ram] to the

FIGURE 5.2

In Inca times, offerings were burned in the courtyard of the House of the Sun
(Coricancha). This space is now the cloister within the Church of Santo Domingo
in Cuzco. (Max T. Vargas, ca. 1930, © President and Fellows of Harvard College,
Peabody Museum of Archaeology and Ethnology, 2004.29.9653.)

hill called Aepiran,[11] because the sun sets behind it, and they would sacrifice it in the same way.[12] Besides these, they would sacrifice and offer to those same *huacas* small baskets with coca, called *paucarrunco* [multicolored basket];[13] ones that they call *paucarquinto* [multicolored cluster], [which were] similar to [those with] coca; small amounts of toasted maize; and red and yellow seashells that they call *mullu* [*Spondylus* shells], carved in the shape of maize.

MAP 5.1
The Cuzco–Vilcanota pilgrimage route. The priests crossed the mountains to reach the Vilcanota pass and then returned to Cuzco by way of the river valley.

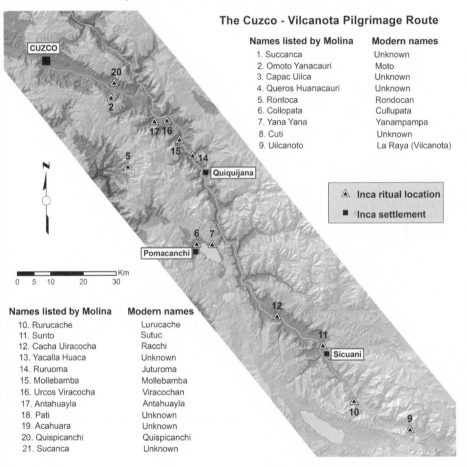

The Cuzco - Vilcanota Pilgrimage Route

Names listed by Molina	Modern names
1. Succanca	Unknown
2. Omoto Yanacauri	Moto
3. Capac Uilca	Unknown
4. Queros Huanacauri	Unknown
5. Rontoca	Rondocan
6. Collopata	Cullupata
7. Yana Yana	Yanampampa
8. Cuti	Unknown
9. Uilcanoto	La Raya (Vilcanota)

△ Inca ritual location
■ Inca settlement

Names listed by Molina	Modern names
10. Rurucache	Lurucache
11. Sunto	Sutuc
12. Cacha Uiracocha	Racchi
13. Yacalla Huaca	Unknown
14. Ruruoma	Juturoma
15. Mollebamba	Mollebamba
16. Urcos Viracocha	Viracochan
17. Antahuayla	Antahuayla
18. Pati	Unknown
19. Acahuara	Unknown
20. Quispicanchi	Quispicanchi
21. Sucanca	Unknown

Likewise, they went to burn the rams and the other things on every day of this month at the following places (Map 5.1):[14] on a hill called Succanca; on another called Omoto Yanacauri;[15] on another called Capac Uilca,[16] which is three leagues from Huanacauri; on another called Queros Huanacauri;[17] on another called Rontoca,[18] which is in Quisguares;[19] on another hill called Collopata,[20] which is in Pomacanche,[21] fourteen leagues from this city; on a plain called Yana Yana;[22] and at another hill called Cuti, which is in the *puna* of Pomacanche. Thus walking, they would go another day to Uilcanoto,[23] which is twenty-six leagues from Cuzco. The reason they followed this road in this month is because they say that the Sun is born in that region.

Thus [on their return to Cuzco], they continued [with] the above-mentioned sacrifices [to the following places]: on a plain that is near Rurucache,[24] they would do the same sacrifice; [and] on another hill called Sunto near Siguana;[25] [and] in Cacha,[26] on another hill called Cacha Uiracocha, they would do the same;[27] [and] on another hill called Yacalla Huaca;[28] [and] on another [place called] Ruruoma,[29] in the plain of Quiquijana;[30] [and] in Mollebamba[31] they would do the same; [and] in Urcos, on a hill called Urcos Viracocha,[32] they would do the same; [and] on a plain that was in Antahuayla,[33] they would burn another [sacrifice]; [and] near Antahuayla, on another [plain] called Pati,[34] they would do the same; [and] on another [plain] called Acahuara,[35] they would do the same; [and] at Quispicanchi,[36] they would do the same on a hill that was there; and at another [hill] called Sucanca,[37] they did the same.

The *tarpuntaes* would go by one road and return by another, and the Inca would go with all the lords to Mantucalla.[38] There he would drink and rest, carrying out his drunken celebrations and *taquis* [dances]. They called this *taqui huallina* [dance chant], and they would perform this dance or song four times a day. Only the Incas participated in this celebration, and those who were in the festivities were served drinks by the *mamaconas*, "women of the Sun." Their own wives did not enter where they were but instead remained outside in a courtyard. All the vessels that they ate and drank from,

FIGURE 5.3

The American Museum of Natural History preserves a silver llama figurine with a red caparison, which was recovered on the Island of the Sun in Lake Titicaca (Bandelier 1910; Bauer and Stanish 2001: 235). This figure is similar, although smaller, to those described by Molina as being used in rituals in Cuzco. (Courtesy of The American Museum of Natural History, #327112 Silver Llama, photograph by Rota.)

and [the] containers in which the food was prepared, were of gold. [When] they performed that *taqui* called *huayllina* [chant], in which they worshipped the Creator, they would bring to this celebration the two female statues called Palpasillo[39] and Inca Oillo. [They were dressed] with very rich clothing covered with gold ornamentation, called *llancapata* [copper disk?], *colcapata* [silver disk?], and *paucar onco* [multicolored tunic]. In front [of them] they would carry the *sunctur paucar* [royal banner] and some large sheep, as big as rams, two of gold and two of silver, which had small red tunics on their backs, in the manner of a caparison (Figure 5.3).[40] They were carried on litters [and] they did so in memory of the [first] ram that they say emerged from Tambo[toco] with them.[41] The Indians who carried them were principal lords, dressed in very rich clothing.[42] They call these gold and silver sheep *cori napa* [gold sacred llama] [and] *colqui napa* [silver sacred llama].[43]

The Inca would stay there in Mantucalla until the end of the month, and when that time arrived, the Inca would go to the plaza called Haucaypata,[44] which is in front of the Cuzco church. The ground over which the Inca was to walk was strewn with bird feathers of every color.[45] He would drink there for the rest of the day and at night he would go to his house. In this way, the month ended.

JUNE

They called the month of June Cauay [or] by another name, Chahuarhuay. They were only occupied in irrigating the *chacras*, and repairing the canals, and carrying the water to sow.[46]

JULY

They called the month of July Moronpassa Tarpuiquilla. In this month they performed the Yahuayra celebrations, during which they asked the Creator for all the food to grow and produce well in that year, and for it to be a prosperous [year]. [This was] because they sowed in this month, in which they held the following ceremonies (Figure 5.4).

The *tarpuntaes*, who are people like priests, were careful to fast from [the time when] they planted the maize until it reached about a finger's height above the ground. They would not have sex with their wives, and their wives and children would also [fast].[47] During this time, they eat nothing but boiled maize and herbs illegible, and they did not drink *chicha* [corn beer], only a clouded [drink] called *concho* [sediment]. Nor did they use coca at this time; they kept a bit of uncooked maize in their *chuspas* [small bags], which they placed in their mouths. In the same way, all the common people participated in the celebration called *llahuayra*, because this is the

FIGURE 5.4

Guaman Poma de Ayala (1980 [1615]: 250 [252]) shows the ritual planting of the first maize that took place in Cuzco. The caption reads "August, month of plowing." Near the bottom of the page is written "time of tilling — the Inca dances the haylli." (Courtesy of Det Kongelige Bibliotek.)

name of the song that was performed, asking the Creator to grant them prosperity. And they did this wearing small red tunics [that hung] down to their feet, without mantles.[48]

They would go to drink and dance[49] at Aucaypata, which the Spaniards now call Limapampa,[50] which is below Santo Domingo. There in the morning, the priests of the Creator would burn a white ram, maize, coca, colored bird feathers, and *mullu*, which, as has been said, are seashells. [While doing this,] they prayed to the Creator to grant a prosperous year, [suggesting that] since he had created everything from nothing and had given them being, he should deem it proper to give them a good year.

Likewise, the sacrifice [items] were given to the priests of the Sun, called *tarpuntaes*, and to the priests of the Thunder so that they would make [the sacrifices] in the same way, praying to the Sun to give warmth so that the crops would grow, as well as to the Thunder, called Chuquiylla, to send his rains, but not hail, so that they would grow. Once these sacrifices were over, the farmers would return to their tilling and the courtiers [would go] to the house of the Lord Inca until the month, which in their language they called *quispe* [crystal],[51] was over.

AUGUST

They called the month of August Coyaraymi and they held the Citua in it.[52] To carry out this celebration they would bring the figures of the *huacas* from all the land, from Quito to Chile, which were placed in the houses [the *huacas*] had in Cuzco, for the purpose that we will describe below. The reason they have this festival called Citua in this month is because that is when the rains begin, and many illnesses tend to occur with the first rains. [Hence, it was] to pray to the Creator to prevent [illnesses] from occurring in Cuzco, as well as in all the [lands] conquered by the Inca, during that year. To perform [the celebration] they would do the following: at noon [on] the day of the conjunction of the Moon, the Inca would go to [the] Coricancha, which is the house and temple of the Sun, with all the men in his council and the most principal Incas that were in Cuzco. They met there to discuss how that festival was to be carried out, because in some years they added or removed [certain aspects] from the festival, [depending on] what they thought was appropriate for the festival.

Thus, the High Priest of the Sun and the Inca, having decided what they would do, everyone left [the Coricancha], and the High Priest announced to the people who were assembled that the Creator deemed it proper for that Citua, or festival, to be held and all the diseases and evils [to be] driven from the land.[53]

For these [festivals], a large number of men armed for war with spears converged and assembled in the plaza[54] that was in front of the temple; [they would be] all prepared for war and [with] their respective squadrons. For this purpose, they would [also] bring to the Temple of the Sun the statues called Chuquilla and Uiracocha, which had their own temples in Pocamarca and Quishuarcancha,[55] and that now are houses that belong to Doña Isabel de Bobadilla.[56] The meeting was conducted with the priests of those *huacas* and [then], with everyone's agreement, the priest of the Sun emerged [from the temple] and announced that festival. Thus with this agreement, they first banished for a distance of two leagues all the foreigners who were not natives of Cuzco;[57] anyone who had broken earlobes;[58] all the hunchbacks; and anyone who had a lesion or defect on their body, saying that they could not attend those festivals because they were deformed by their own fate, and that it was not right for unlucky people to be there, since their misfortune would hinder good fortune. They also would drive out the dogs of the town so that they would not howl. Then those men who were prepared for war would leave for the plaza of Cuzco and would shout out, "Illnesses, disasters, misfortunes, and dangers, leave this land!"

In the middle of the plaza, where the gold *usño* [ceremonial platform][59] was, which was like a well into which they poured the *chicha*[60] sacrifice when they drank, [the initial runners] would encounter four hundred Indians ready for war surrounding the well. One hundred faced toward Collasuyo, which is to the east; another one hundred faced the west, which is [toward] the road of Chinchaysuyo; another one hundred faced north, which is [toward] the road of Antisuyo; and one hundred faced the south, [which is toward Cuntisuyo].[61] They had [with them] all the kinds of weapons they used.

As soon as those who were coming from the Temple of the Sun arrived, they all cried out, "Evil, be gone!" and all four squadrons would leave, each toward their appointed region (Map 5.2; Table 5.1).[62] Those who were [going] to Collasuyo would go with great haste to the straits of Acoyapongo,[63] which is about two short leagues from Cuzco, and they would shout, "Evil, be gone!" The men of Hurin Cuzco would take these shouts [until they arrived] there, where they would deliver the [shouts] to the *mitimas* of Huayparya,[64] who would deliver them to the *mitimas* of Antahuaylla.[65] The *mitimas* of

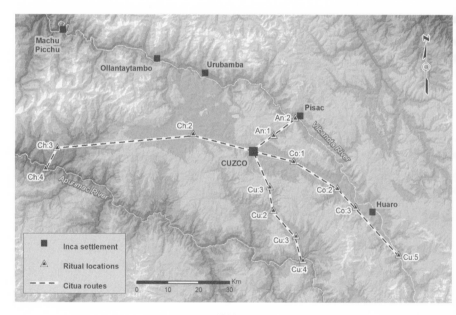

MAP 5.2

During the Citua, runners would leave Cuzco and travel into the four quarters of the Inca heartland. The runners organized themselves into relays and carried the ritual materials to the major rivers of the region. The runners then bathed and washed their weapons in the rivers. Through this action, Cuzco was cleansed and the maladies of the city were carried away.

TABLE 5.1. Locations Mentioned in Molina's Account of the Citua

Names Listed by Molina	Modern Name	Distance from Cuzco
Collasuyo		
Co: 1. Acoyapongo	Angostura	14 km
Co: 2. Huaypar	Huacarpay ?	30 km
Co: 3. Antahuaylla	Andahuaylillas	38 km
Co: 4. Huaraypacha	Unknown	—
Co: 5. Quiquijana	Vilcanota River near Quiquijana	64 km
Chinchaysuyo		
Ch: 1. Satpina	Unknown	
Ch: 2. Jaquejahuana	Xaquixahuana	18 km
Ch: 3. Tilca	Tilca	65 km
Ch: 4. Apurimac	Apurimac River	70 km
Antisuyo		
An: 1. Chita	Chitapampa	9 km
An: 2. Pisa[c]	Vilcanota River near Pisac	19 km
Cuntisuyo		
Cu: 1. Churicalla	Churicalla	7 km
Cu: 2. Yaurisque	Yaurisque	9 km
Cu: 2. Tantar	Tantar Cuzco	35 km
Cu: 3. Cusibamba	Apurimac River near Cusibamba	41 km

Antahuaylla would deliver the [shouts] to the *mitimas* of Huarayapa-cha,[66] and these would take them to the Quiquijana River.[67] There they would wash themselves and the weapons they carried. In this way [the journey] was completed in this area [of Collasuyo]. The Indians who left Cuzco and carried the shouts toward Collasuyo were from the lineages of Uscaymata *ayllo* [kin group], Yapomayho *ayllo*, Yahuaymin *ayllo*, Sutic [*ayllo*], Maras *ayllo*, [and] Cuyuissa *ayllo*.[68]

Those who would depart for the west, which is toward Chinchaysuyo, would leave shouting in the same way. They were from the lineages of Capac *ayllo*, Atun *ayllo*, Uicaquicao [*ayllo*], Chaueticuzco *ayllo*, Arayraca *ayllo*, and others [were] from Uro [*ayllo*].[69] These would carry the shouts until Satpina,[70] which is a little more than a league from Cuzco. They would deliver [the shouts] to the *mitimas* of Jaquejahuana,[71] and they would deliver them to the *mitimas* of Tilca,[72] which is above Marcahuaçi,[73] almost ten leagues from Cuzco. These [*mitimas*] would take [the shouts] to the Apurimac River and there they would throw them [into the river], bathing themselves and washing their wools[74] and weapons.[75]

Those who carried the shouts to the area of Antisuyo belonged to the following lineages: Xusçu Panaca *ayllo*, Aucaylli *ayllo*, Tarpuntai *ayllo*, [and] Saño *ayllo*.[76] These would take the [shouts] to Chita,[77] which is a league and a half from Cuzco, and they would deliver them to the *mitimas* of Pisa[c],[78] who are from the Cuyo and Paullo.[79] These [*mitimas*] took them to the Pisac River, and there they jumped in and bathed and washed their weapons.[80]

Those who went to the area to the area [*sic*] of Cuntisuyo belonged to the following lineages: Raura Panaca *ayllo*, China Panaca *ayllo*, Masca Panaca *ayllo*, and Quesco *ayllo*.[81] These would take [the shouts] to Churicalla,[82] which is two leagues from Cuzco, and there they would deliver them to the *mitimas* of Yaurisque,[83] which is three leagues from Cuzco. These delivered [the shouts] to those of Tantar,[84] which is four leagues from Cuzco, and these would take them to the Cusibamba River, where the friars of La Merced have a vineyard, which is seven leagues from Cuzco.[85] There they would bathe and wash their weapons.

This is how they performed the ceremony to drive illnesses out of Cuzco. The reason that they bathed in these rivers was because these are voluminous rivers [that] they know lead to the sea, and so the [rivers] would carry the illnesses [away].[86] When the shouting began in Cuzco, everyone from large and small [blank space][87] would appear at their door, shaking mantles and *llicllas* [mantles], saying, "Evil, be gone! Oh, what a long-awaited celebration this has been for us! O Creator of All Things, grant us another year so that we can see another celebration like this one!"[88] During that [night], they would all dance, including the Inca. And at dawn, everyone would go to the springs and rivers to bathe in twilight, ordering the

FIGURE 5.5

An important element of the Citua ritual were large straw balls that were set on fire. Guaman Poma de Ayala (1980 [1615]: 252–253) describes their use in the following: "And in this month the Incas ordered that the sicknesses and pestilence be cast out of all the towns in the kingdom. Men armed as if they were going to fight a war, throwing fire slings, saying in a loud voice, 'Leave sicknesses and pestilences from the people and from this town! Leave us!'" (Courtesy of Det Kongelige Bibliotek.)

illnesses to leave them. After they bathed, they would take some large straw torches, like very large balls, which they would tie with some ropes and light them [on fire].[89] They would go about playing with them or, more precisely, hitting one another. They called these straw balls *mauro pancunco* (Figure 5.5).

Once that was over, they would go to their houses, and by then they would have a mixture of coarsely ground maize prepared, which they called *sanco* [maize paste].[90] They would place its [blank space][91] on their faces, also smearing it on the lintels of the doors, and in the places where they kept their food and clothes. They would also take the *sanco* to the springs and throw it in, asking not to be ill or for the illnesses [not] to enter any given house. They would also send this *sanco* to their relatives and friends for the same purpose, and they would warm the bodies of the dead with it [as well], so that they could enjoy the celebration.

And then with much rejoicing, they would eat and drink the best foods they had, since each person, even the poorest, would have saved [blank space] things to eat and drink for this day. [They did so] because they said that [on] this day, [anyone who] did not rest, eat, and drink would be unlucky and would have hardships in both work and life during the [following] year. During this [celebration] time, they would not argue with one another, nor would they speak angry words, nor would they ask one another to repay their debts, because they said that if they started on this day, they would have quarrels and difficulties all year long.

That night they would also bring out the statues of the Sun, Creator, and Thunder, and the priests of each one of the statues would warm them with the mentioned *sanco*. The next morning they would bring to the temple[s] of the Creator, Sun, and Thunder the very finest and best seasoned foods ever to present to [the statues]. The priests of the *huacas* would receive these [foods] and burn them. They would also take out the embalmed bodies[92] of the dead lords and ladies, which were brought by the persons of their lineage who were in charge of them. And that night they would wash them in their baths that each had [used] while alive. Once they were returned to their houses, they were warmed with *çanco* [maize paste], the thick mixture that has been mentioned. They would place in front of the [dead rulers] the foods that each had used and enjoyed eating the most when they were alive, and these were well seasoned, like when they were alive. Then the people who were in charge of the dead [rulers] would burn [these foods].

The servants who were in charge of the *huaca* called Huanacauri, which is a large stone [in the] shape of [a] man, together with its priest, would wash that *huaca*[93] and warm it with the *sanco*. And as soon as the principal Inca lord finished bathing, [he] and his principal wife would go to their chamber, and [others] would place *sanco* on their heads on their heads [*sic*]. After they were warmed with it, they would put some feathers from a bird that is called *pielco*, which are iridescent in color, [on their heads]. The same was done with the statue of the Creator by those who were in charge of it. They used to call this ceremony *pil[c]oyaco* [*pilco* feather diadem].

Later, about eight or nine in the morning, the principal Inca lord, with his wife and [the] courtiers of his council whom he had in his house, would go as richly dressed as possible to the main plaza of Cuzco (Figure 5.6).[94] At this same time, they would bring to the plaza the image of the Sun called Apin Punchao, which was the principal [idol] that they had in their temple, accompanied by all the priests of the Sun, together with the two gold images called Ynca Ocllo [Inca noble women] and Palpa Ocllo [noble women],[95] [which were] its wives. The woman called Coya Pacssa [Queen Moon] was also brought out. She was dedicated as wife of the Sun, and was [a] sister [or] daughter of the ruler.

The priests would bring out the Sun [image] and place it on the seat that was dedicated for it in the plaza. In the same way, the priests of the Creator would bring out its statue to the plaza, where they would set it in its place. The priests of the Thunder, called Chuquiylla, would also bring out its statue, which they would set in its place in the plaza.

The [statues] had their gold benches [and] in front of them they had their *yauris* [staffs], which were like gold scepters. For this

FIGURE 5.6

The central plaza of Cuzco. In Inca times, the plaza was much larger. (Photograph by Max Vargas, ca. 1930, private collection.)

celebration, the priests of the *huacas* would come with their finest clothes. Likewise, those who were in charge of the Huanacauri *huaca* would bring out its statue and set it set it [*sic*] in the plaza, in the place they had for it. They say that they never gave the *huaca* of the Creator its own wife because they say the Creator did not want wives, since he had created everything. They say that all was his. Thus in all their sacrifices they [always] offered the first one to the Creator.

At the same time, they would also bring out the very richly dressed embalmed bodies of all the lords and ladies. Their bodies were cared for by the descendants of their lineages that were in charge of them. They would place them on their gold seats in the plaza, according to their order, as if they were alive. At this time, everyone in Cuzco would come out according to their *ayllos* and groups. They [all] would come as richly dressed as they could, and on arriving, they made obeisance[96] to the Creator, the Sun, and the Lord Inca. Afterward, they would sit in their seats, each one according to the status they had, [thus] dividing the Hanan Cuzcos [Upper Cuzcos] on their side and the Hurin Cuzcos [Lower Cuzcos] on theirs.⁹⁷ They would dedicate this day only to eat, drink, and amuse themselves. They would also perform the *taqui* called *alaui citua taqui* [Citua dance song] with some small red tunics [that reached] their feet and some diadems called *pilco casa* [*pilco* feather diadem]⁹⁸ on their heads. They would also play some short and long cane flutes, playing a music called *tica tica* with them.

On that day they would give thanks to the Creator for having allowed them to be alive for that [year's] celebration and they [would ask him] to grant them another year without illnesses. [They expressed] the same to the Sun and the Thunder, and the Inca would drink with them. The Sun had in front of it a large gold vessel in which the Inca would pour *chicha*. The priest would take it from there and pour it into the *usñu* [ceremonial platform],⁹⁹ which, as has been said, is like a stone well, covered in gold. It had a hole made in such a way that the flow [of *chicha*] would reach a drain that went underground until the Houses of the Sun, the Thunder, and the Creator.¹⁰⁰ Their priests would drink with one another, and the embalmed bodies of [H]anan Cuzco [would drink] with those of Hurin Cuzco (Figure 5.7). And in this way they passed and spent that day in the above-mentioned [activities]. Once the evening came, those who were in charge of them would take the Sun and the other *huacas* to their temples, and the embalmed bodies to their houses. The Inca and the rest of the people would go to their lodgings.

The next day they would go to the same plaza, in the same order. And with the *huacas*, the Inca, and the other people arranged in their order, the [people] would bring to the plaza an enormous quantity of livestock, of all types, from each of the four regions, [which are] called Collasuyo, Chinchaysuyo, Antisuyo, and Cuntisuyo. According to what is said by those who gave statements, the quantity of livestock was so great that there were over one hundred thousand heads. This livestock had to be clean, without any blemishes or marks, and woolly, having never been shorn. Then the priest of the Sun would set aside four rams, the cleanest ones, and

FIGURE 5.7

During the major celebrations of Cuzco, the mummies of the dead kings and queens would be brought to the plaza and the ruling Inca would drink with them. (Drawing by Guaman Poma de Ayala (1980 [1615]: 287 [289].) (Courtesy of Det Kongelige Bibliotek.)

he would sacrifice them in this manner: one to the Creator, another to the Thunder, another to the Sun, and the other one to Huanacauri. When these sacrifices were to be carried out, they had some large gold plates holding *sanco*. [And the priests] would spray that *sanco* with the blood of the rams that were sacrificed. The white and woolly rams were called *cuyllo* [white].[101] The plates that [held] the *sanco* were in front of the bench of the Sun, and the High Priest would speak out, so that all could hear:

> Beware how you eat this *sanco*, for he who eats it in sin and with two wills and [two] hearts will be seen and punished by the Sun, our Father, and will suffer great hardships. But he who eats it with an unbroken spirit will be rewarded by the Creator, the Sun, and the Thunder; and [they] will give you children, joyful years, bountiful food, and everything else needed for success.

Then [they] would rise to take [the *sanco*], first making a solemn oath before eating the *yahuarcanco* [blood paste].[102] With this [oath] they promised, on pain of condemnation and hardships, to never be or speak against the Creator, nor the Sun, nor the Thunder; or to betray the Inca, their principal Lord.

The priest of the Sun [would use] three fingers to take as much of the [*sanco*] as he wanted from the plate. He would put it in his mouth and then return to his seat. Following this example, and with this type of oath, the groups[103] rose, and [the *sanco*] was given to everyone in this way, even to the babies. They would save [part] of the *yahuarsanco* [blood paste] for those who were absent and they would send it to the sick who were in their beds, because anyone who was not able[104] to receive the *yahuarsanco* [blood paste] on that day was seen as very unfortunate. They did this with such care that no crumb would fall on the ground because they held as [a] great sin that it would [blank space].

When they killed the rams mentioned above, they took out the lungs, which they inflated by blowing [into] them. Once inflated, the priests would look for certain signs that were in them, indicating if everything in the forthcoming year would be prosperous or not. Then they would burn the lungs in front of the Creator, the Sun, and the Thunder. They would divide the [sacrificed] rams' bodies as a sacred thing, [giving] a little to each [priest]. All the rest of the livestock was divided among all the people of Cuzco for them to eat. And as they entered the plaza, each [person] tore off a piece of wool used in their sacrifices to the Sun. When dividing the livestock, the priests would say the following prayers:

FIRST PRAYER TO THE CREATOR[105]

A ticsi uiracochan caylla uiracochan tocapo acnupo uiracochan camachurac cari cachon huarmi cachon ñispa llutac rurac camascayque churascaiqui casilla quespilla cauçamusac maipim canqui ahuapichu cocupichu puyupichu llantupichu hoyarihuay hayniguai y nihuai y maypachacama haycaypachacama cauçachihuay marcarihuay hatallihuay cay cuzcaitari chasquihuay maypis capapos uiracochaya.

Translation of this prayer:[106]

O Creator! [You] who are without equal to the end of the world. [You] who gave life and strength to mankind, and said, "[Let] this one be male," and to the women, "[Let] this one be female." Saying this, you created them, shaped them, and gave them life. Protect those that you have created, [let them] live safe and sound, without danger, [and] in peace. Where are you? Are you in the heights of heaven? Or below in the thunder [clouds]? Or in the storm clouds? Hear me, answer me, and grant me [my prayers]; give us eternal life forever. Take us by your hand and receive this offering wherever you may be, O Creator![107]

Another prayer so that the people can multiply:

Viracochan apacochan titu uiracochan hualpaihuana uiracochan
topapo acnupo viracochan runa yachachuchun huarma yachachu-
chur mirachun llacta pacha casilla quispilla cachun camascayquita
guacaychay atalliymay pachacama haycay pachacama.

Translation of this prayer:

O Creator! [You] who do wonders and things never before
seen. Most merciful Creator without measure, [let] the people
multiply and have offspring. [Let] the towns and lands be without dangers, and protect those to whom you gave being and
take them by the hand, forever and ever.

[A PRAYER] TO ALL THE *HUACAS*

Caylla uiracochan ticçi uiracochan hapacochan hualpaihuana
uiracochan chanca uiracocham acxa uiracochan atun uiracochan
caylla uiracochan tacancuna aynichic hunichic llacta runa yacha-
cuc capac hahuaypi hucupi purispapas.

Translation:[108]

Creator, [you] who are at the end of the world, Chanca Uiracochan (which is a *huaca* that is in Chuquichaca,[109] where Manco
Inca was), Atun Uiracochan (which is in the *huaca* of Urcos;
at the entrance of this *huaca* were stone statues of an eagle
and a hawk,[110] and inside was a statue of [a] man, with a small
white tunic reaching [his] feet, and his hair reaching his waist;
the statues of the eagle and hawk chirped each day at noon
as if they were alive. The *camayos* [specialists] said that they
chirped because Uiracocha was hungry and they took food to
them, which they burned; they say that they were [the] sons
and brothers of this Urcos Uiracochan), Apotin Uiracochan
(which is in Amaybamba[111] beyond [Ollantay]tambo), Urusayua Uiracocha ([which is] in the same town), Chuquichanca

Uiracochan ([which] is in Huaypon[112]). You [huacas] grant the Creator, who is at the end of the world [blank space], that the people and lands be always prosperous, going with the Creator, whether inside or outside of heaven.

Another prayer:

O uiracochan cusi ussapoc hayllipo uiracochaya runa caya mayda caymi runa yana huaccha quisa runayqui camascayqui çhurascayqui casi quispilla camuchun huarmay huan churinhuan chincanta amaguatquintaguan yayaichichu unay huasa causachun mana allcas pa mana pitispa micumuchun upiamuchun.

Translation:

O Creator, most joyful, most fortunate Creator! You who are merciful and pitiful to men. Observe here your poor, unfortunate men and servants, who you made and gave being. Take pity on them. [Let them] live safe and sound with their children and descendants. [Let them] walk the straight path, without contemplating evil deeds. [Let them] live long lives, not die young, [and] live and eat in peace.[113]

Another prayer:

O uiracochaya ticçi uiracochaya hualparillac camac çhurac cay hurin pachapen micuchun upiachun ñispa churascayquicta camascayquicta micuinin yachachun papa cara ymaymana miconcan cachon ñiscayqueta camachic micachic mana muchuncanpaç mana muchuspa canta yñincampac ama caçachuncho ama chupichichuncho casilla huacaychamuy.

Translation:

O Creator! Lord to the end of the world. Merciful one. You

who give being to everything. You who enable men to eat and drink in this world. Increase their [blank space] and fruits of the earth, potatoes and all the other foods that you created; multiply [them] so that [people] do not suffer hunger or misery [and] so that they will reproduce. Let it not frost or hail. Keep them in safety and in peace.

PRAYER TO THE SUN

Uiracochaya punchao cachun tota cachun ñispac nic pacarichun yllarichun ñispac nic punchao churiyquicta casillacta quispillacta purichic runa rurascayquicta can canchay vn cancampac viracochaya.

Casilla quispilla punchao ynga runa yana miohiscayquicta quillari canchari ama honcochispa ama nanachispa caçita quispicha huacaychaspa.

Translation of this prayer:

O Creator! [You] who gave being to the Sun and then said, "[Let] there be night and day, dawn and sunshine." [Let the Sun] rise in peace and protect it so that it can shed light on the people that you created, O Creator!

O Sun! [You] who are in safety and in peace, shed light on those people whom you watch over. [Protect them] from illness. Keep [them] safe and sound.

PRAYER FOR [THE] INCA

A uiracochan ticçi uiracochan gualpayhuana uiracochan atun uiracochan tarapaca uiracochan capac cachun ynca cachun nispac ñucapac churaspacquecta ynca camascayquicta casillacta quispollacta huacaychamuy runan yanan yachachuchun aoca ripunari vsachun ymay pacha haycaypacha cama ama allcachispa churinta mitantaquanpas huacaychachay caçic cac llacta uiracochaya.

Translation:

> O Merciful Creator! [You] who are at the end of the world, who ordered and deemed it proper for there to be a Lord Inca. Keep this Inca, whom you created, in safety and in peace along with his servants and vassals. [Let] him have victories over his enemies [and] always be victorious. Do not shorten his days or those of his sons or descendants. Keep them in peace, O Creator!

Another prayer:

> *Uiracochaya gualpayhuana uiracochaya runacta casi quispillacta capac ynga churiyqui guarmayquipas camascayqui huacaychamuchun hatallimuchun pacha chacarra runa llama micuy pay captin yacochun capac ynca camascayquicta uiracochaya ayni huñi marcari hatalli ymay pachacama.*

Translation of this prayer:

> O Creator! [Let] the people, towns, and the subjects of the Inca and his servants be safe and in peace during the time of your son the Inca, whom you made a Lord. During his reign, [let the people] multiply and remain safe, [and keep] the times prosperous, and [let] the *chacras*, people, and livestock increase. Take the Lord [Inca], to whom you gave being [blank space], by your hand forever, O Creator!

Another prayer:

> *Pachamama casillacta quispillacta capac ynca huahuayquicta marcari atalli.*

Translation of this prayer:

O Mother Earth, hold your son the Inca over you, calm and in peace.[114]

PRAYER FOR ALL THE INCAS

A punchao ynca inti yayay cuzco tambo cachon aticoc llasacoc ca-chun ñispa churac camac muchascayqui cu siquispo canchon ama-tisca [blank space].

Ama llasasca caçhuncho aticucpac llasa capac camascayqui churascayqui.

Translation:

O Sun! My Father who said, "Let there be Cuzcos and Tam-bos."[115] [Let] these sons of yours be victorious and despoilers of all peoples. [I] pray to you so these Incas, your sons, are blessed [and will] not be vanquished or despoiled, but rather will al-ways be victorious, since you made them for this.[116]

PRAYER TO ALL THE *HUACAS*

O pacha chulla vnacochan ocu chulla uiracochan huaca uilca ca-chun nispa camac atun apa huaypihuana tayna allasto allonto uiracochaya hurin pacha anan pacha cachon nispa nic ocu pachapi puca omacta churac hayniguai huniguay quispi casi camusac uira-cochaya micuynioc mincacyoc carayoc llamayoc ymaynayoc hay-caymayoc ama caçharihuaycuchu ymaymana aycaymara chiqui-manta catuimanmanta nacasca huatusca amuscamanta.[117]

Translation:

O fathers, *huacas* and *huillcas* ancestors, grandfathers, and our fathers, *atun apa hualpi huana tayna apo allasto allento,*[118] bring the Creator close to your sons, to your children, and to your offspring. Give your sons being so that they can be blessed alongside the Creator, as you are.[119]

And thus [having] divided the livestock, they killed a large number to eat on that day. Then they brought into the plaza a great quantity of *chicha*, which had been prepared much earlier and kept in storage houses that they had for this purpose. [The *chicha*] was made from white maize harvested in the Cuzco Valley. The livestock for this celebration were taken from the herds of the Creator, Sun, and Thunder, which they kept distributed across all the provinces of Peru. And after eating with much rejoicing, they performed their *taquis*, and they drank in the [same] order as the previous day. [All] this lasted four days. The first day of this festival called Citua was when they ate the aforementioned *sanco* [called] *yaguarcanco* [blood paste]. They dedicated the second day to the Creator, Sun, and Thunder, making sacrifices for them and [saying] the aforementioned prayer for the Inca. The fourth day[120] [was] for the Moon and the Earth, [during which] they carried out their accustomed sacrifices and prayers to them.

The next day in the morning, all the nations that the Inca had subjected would enter [the plaza]. They came with their *huacas* and dressed in the clothing of their lands, the finest that they could have. And the priests who were in charge of the *huacas* carried them on litters.[121] Reaching the plaza, they entered according to their areas from the four *suyos* [regions], and offered reverence to the Creator, Sun, Thunder, [and] Huanacauri, [which was the] *huaca* of the Incas, and then to the Inca, who by that time was already in the plaza. In this way, they would go arrange themselves in their previously assigned positions. To provide them with more space, the Indians of [H]anan Cuzco and Hurin Cuzco combined both groups into one and thus made more space in the plaza. Once they were all situated in their positions, the High Priest of the Sun would come out and call for a great quantity of *sanco* in the aforementioned way. And while he sprayed it with blood, the *caciques* [local lords] would begin to stand up according to their order, saying the following prayer to the Creator:

A ticçi uiracochan caylla uiracochan tocapo acnupo uiracochan

camac churac cari cachun guarmi caçhun nispa llutac rurac camas-
cayqui chorascayqui casilla quispilla caussamusai maypin canqui
ahuapichu ucupichu llantupichu oyariguai ayniguay yniguay ymay
pachamama cauçachihuay marcalliguai atalliguay cay coscaytari
chasquihuay maypi caspapas uiracochaya.

Translation:

O Creator! [You] who are at the ends of the world [and have] no
equal. [You] who gave being and valor to men and said, "[Let]
this one be male," and to the women, "[Let] this one be female."
Saying this, you created them, shaped them, and gave them life.
Protect them and [let them] live safe and sound, without danger, living in peace. Where are you? Are you in the heights of
heaven, below in the clouds, or in the storm clouds? Hear us,
answer us, grant us [our prayers], and give us eternal life. Take
us by your hand forever and receive this offering [blank space]
wherever you may be, O Creator![122]

And then the priest of the Sun, having taken the oaths [of the *caciques*] in the manner already mentioned and having already taken
the vow, [he] would give them the *yahuarcanco* [blood paste] in
the above-mentioned order. Once that was finished, they would eat
the meat of the ram that had been sacrificed to the Creator, Sun,
and Thunder. Each nation spent this day doing the *taqui*, song and
dance, that each had performed in their lands before they were subjected by the Inca.

On this day, everyone who had been driven out of Cuzco because of their physical defects joined the festival [and] these would
be found again in the festival. This celebration lasted for two days,
at the end of which, at dusk, they burned a ram in sacrifice and a
great quantity of clothing of all colors. Those who had to return to
their lands asked the Creator, the Sun, the Thunder, and the Inca for
permission [to depart]. They would grant it as long as they [blank
space] left the *huacas* that they had brought that year as a gift in

Cuzco and took and returned to their lands the ones they had left during the festival the previous year. They were given gold, silver, cloth, women, and servants as a reward for the effort they had made in coming from such distant lands. And the principal lords were given permission to travel in litters. They [also] gave the *huacas chacras* in their lands and servants to serve them. They burned the foods that they harvested and performed their sacrifices. In this way they would all return to their homelands.

Inca Yupanqui was the inventor of this celebration, [ordering] it to be performed in the above-mentioned way. Because although it was carried out before [his rule], since there have been Incas, it has been performed in a different way. They would spend the remainder of the month doing whatever they wanted or what was convenient for them. In the same way, all the Inca governors and [those] belonging to their lineage would hold this festival or holy period,[123] called *citua*, in all the provincial capitals. [They did it] wherever they were [at the proper date] and for the proper length, although with less solemnity and fewer sacrifices, but not because they omitted any of the rites.[124]

SEPTEMBER

They called the month of September Omac Raymi. They called it that way because [during it] the Indians of Oma,[125] which is two leagues from Cuzco, held the *guarachillo* [male initiation rite] festival, which is when they armed the youths as warriors[126] and pierced their ears, as will be described in its [proper] place. In Cuzco, the women who had sons whose ears were to be pierced and [who were to] undergo the *guarachico* [male initiation rite] occupied themselves weaving the clothes that their sons were to wear on the day of the *guarachico* [male initiation rite] festival. Some members of their lineage gathered to help them weave, drink, and rest for some days in their houses. Each of the males occupied themselves in the [tasks that] the Inca had him working on. And so the month would end in this way.

They called the month of October Ayarmaca Raymi. It was named this way because the Indians of the town of Ayarmaca[127] held the *guarachico* [male initiation rite] celebrations [during it] and pierce the ears [of] the youths of that town and arm [them as] warriors, according to their customs with the ceremonies that will be described ahead. So as not to make [this work] lengthy, I will not describe them [here].

In Cuzco, they would occupy themselves making a great quantity of *chicha* for the celebration that was to be held, called Capac Raymi. They called this method of making *chicha cantaray.*[128] And the youths that were to be armed as warriors would go to the *huaca* called Huanacauri to offer [it] sacrifices and to ask [for] its permission to arm themselves as warriors. [They would do so, holding it] as their principal *huaca*, which they said was the brother of Manco Capac, from whom they say they descended. So as to not make [this report] lengthy, I will not discuss the fable of this *huaca* here, having [already] made reference to it in the *History of the Incas* that I have done.[129] [I will] just [say] that the youths that were to be armed as warriors would sleep that night on the hill of Huanacauri, where the *huaca* was, reenacting the pilgrimage that their ancestors had undertaken from there.

They would return [to Cuzco] the next day in the afternoon, bringing a load of straw so that their fathers and other relatives could sit on [it]. The youths fasted on this day, and so during this month they also made many varieties of *chicha* and the necessary preparations for the festival.[130] During this time and always, the priests of the Creator, Sun, Thunder, and those who were in charge of the *huaca* of Huanacauri performed their sacrifices three times a day, without fail. They would burn three rams: one in the morning, one at noon, and another in the evening, along with other foods that were assigned for that purpose. [They] believed that the *huacas* ate that [food] wherever they were. The [priests] would take the foods to the above-mentioned hills during the Inti Raymi festival. Also, the people who were in charge of the embalmed bodies never missed a day to burn the foods and pour the *chicha* that were assigned for that [purpose]. [These were prepared] in the way the [deceased] used to eat [them] when they were alive. They would burn the foods that [the deceased] used to eat while they were alive, because they understood and held the immortality of the soul as a great truth. And they said that wherever the soul was, it would receive the [offering] and would eat it as if it were alive. In this way the month ended.

NOVEMBER

They called the month of November Capac Raymi, which means "festival of the Lord Inca."[131] [This] was one of the most important celebrations of the year [and] one of the three main festivals that they performed (Figure 5.8). In this month, they would arm [the] warriors, pierce their ears, and give them loincloths, which in their language they call *guara*.[132] For this festival and [to] arm the warriors, all the parents and relatives of those who were to be armed as warriors worked during the first eight days of the month to make *ojotas* [sandals], which were shoes. [They were] made from a very thin straw that they call *ooja* [*sic; qoya* = grass], [which] looks almost like the color of gold.[133] They [also worked] making *guaracas* [slings] of ram sinews, which were made to be used [in the festival], and sewing the fringes onto the tunics that they were to use to go to the *huaca* called Huanacauri. [They called these] *chumpi caçico* [chestnut brown tunic?], [which] were tunics made out of fine dark brown wool with fine black wo[ol] fringes that looked like silk, [measuring] just over a palm and a half. [They would also make] some long and narrow white wool mantles that they call *supa yacolla* [tail scarf], [which] were no more than two palms wide and [which] hung to their knees. These were tied with a knot at the neck, from where a cord of wool, which ended with a red tassel, came out. The *llaytos* [headbands] that they would wear on that day were black [and] adorned.[134]

FIGURE 5.8

Capac Raymi was one of the most important celebrations of the Incas. Guaman Poma de Ayala depicts this celebration taking place in Cuzco. The caption reads "December Royal Sun Celebration." Near the bottom of the page is written "The great solemn holy period of the Sun." (Drawing by Guaman Poma de Ayala [1980 (1615): 258 (260)].) (Courtesy of Det Kongelige Bibliotek.)

On the morning of the ninth day, everyone, including the fathers as well as the relatives of those who were to be armed as warriors, would go to the plaza. The fathers and relatives would arrive dressed in some vestments that they call *collca onco* [silver-bangled tunic?]. Depending on [which part of] the celebrations they performed, there were differences in the clothes they wore. The tan mantles and the black feathers on their heads were from a bird that they call *quito*. Accordingly, they called the [headdress] *quitotica* [feathers of the *quito*]. And those who were to be armed as warriors were shorn.[135] After shearing them, they would put on the clothes mentioned above.

[A] large number of maidens, who were assigned and chosen to serve in that celebration, would arrive at the plaza that day, dressed in clothes that they call *cuzco axo* [Cuzco skirt] and *cochelli* [unknown term] *quilla* [moon]. They were eleven, twelve, and fourteen [years] old [and] were of high status. They were called *ñusta callixapa* [health princess], [and] they served to carry some small jugs of *chicha*, and to wait with them at rest stops, as will be described below. And [with] everyone dressed as has been said, they would go with their fathers and relatives to the House of the Sun and [the House of the] Thunder, and bring the [statues] to the plaza, where they were placed. Then the Inca would emerge and sit in his place, next to the statue of the Sun. Those who were to be armed as warriors would rise and each would go successively, performing the *mucha* [veneration], which is a form of obeisance paid to the *huacas*.[136] They would also bring out a statue of a woman, which was the *huaca* of the Moon, which they called Passa Mama [Mother Moon]. Women were in charge of it. Thus, when they came out of the House of the Sun, where it had its own abode, where the balcony of Santo Domingo is now, [the women] would carry out [the *huaca*] on [their] shoulders. The reason women were in charge of it [was] because they said [the moon] was a woman, as portrayed by her statue.[137] Once the mentioned obeisance [was] done, they would stay quiet for a while, until it was noon. When it seemed to them that it was [noon], they performed their obeisance to the *hua-*

cas again and they asked permission from the Inca to go to make their sacrifices, in the following way.

Each of those who were to be armed in this way as warriors had already prepared a ram to sacrifice. They would go with them, and with members of their lineage, to the hill called Huanacauri and sleep that day in a place at the foot of the hill called Matahua.[138] The next day at sunrise, which was the tenth day, [and having] all fasted because they would fast that day, they would climb the hill until they reached the *huaca* of Huanacauri. They would leave the sheep that they had taken for the sacrifice at the foot of the hill in Matahua. The *tarpuntaes*, who are the priests who were to conduct the sacrifice, would take a bit of wool from each one. Thus, when everyone reached the top, the *tarpuntaes* would take five lambs and burn them in front of that *huaca*. They would also divide the wool that they carried in their hands among the young men who were to be armed as warriors and the *caciques* [local lords] who used to go there. They blew it into the air, saying these words while the sacrifice burned:

> O Huanacauri! Our father. [Let] the Creator, Sun, Thunder, and Moon be forever young and never age. And [let] the Inca, your son, be forever young and may he succeed in all that he does. And Creator, Sun, Thunder, Moon, and you [Huanacauri], hold us, your children and descendants, who now make this celebration for you [Huanacauri], in your hands forever and give us all that is needed for our household[s].

In the ninth hour of the day, [once] the sacrifice [was] concluded, they would hand them the *guaracas* [slings] and some bunches of straw[139] called *chuspas* [small bags]. Having given them the *guaracas*, they told them this, "So, our father Huanacauri has given you the *guaracas* of brave and safe [men]; live as honest people." Saying these phrases, the High Priest of that *huaca* handed them the *guaracas*. These were made of ram sinews and *chaguar* [maguey] [fibers], which is like flax. This was done because they said that their ances-

tors, when they left Pacaritambo, had also carried them like this.[140]
Then they would go to a ravine that was called Quirasmanta.[141]
There, the uncles, fathers, and *curacas* [local lords] would, in [the]
name of the *huacas*, flog the [youths] on their arms and legs with
the *guaracas* that they had been given, saying: "Be as brave and as
good of a man as I have been. May you receive the graces that I have
so that you can emulate me." Later in this place, they would sing a
song called *guari*, during which the armed warriors stood with the
bunches of straw in their hands and all the rest of the people sat.[142]

[When] that *taqui* was finished, they would rise and start for
Cuzco, where a shepherd among those who were in charge [of] certain livestock, called *raymi napa* [ritual sacred llama], which were
dedicated for this festival, would come to the road to meet them.
They brought a ram called *napa* [sacred llama], which had [a cloth]
similar to a red tunic over it and gold ear [tassels]. They came with
the sheep, playing [music] with some drilled seashells, called *gayllaiquipac* [shell trumpet].[143] Also, an Indian would bring the *suntur
paucar* [royal banner], which was [an] insignia of the Lord [Inca].
Having arrived with all these [items] where the people were, they
would perform a dance and [when] finished, they would leave carrying that sheep and [the] *suntur paucar* [royal banner] in front of
them. Everyone would go by their [respective] groups and *ayllos*
until they reached Cuzco. Those who had been armed as warriors
would carry the *guaracas* [slings] on their head and the straw bunches in their hands. When they reached the plaza, they would offer
obeisance to the already-mentioned *huacas*. Once they finished,
the fathers, uncles, and relatives would flog them on their arms and
legs and then all the people would perform the *taqui* called *guari*.
That finished, all the youths gave their fathers, uncles, and relatives
who had beaten them something to drink. By this time it was almost
night, so they would go to their houses, where they ate the sacrificial
rams, and the priests would return the *huacas* to their temples.

Having finished [blank space], the following days they did
nothing more than rest in their homes. And the youths who had
been armed as warriors rested from the past events and prepared for

the future ones. On the fourteenth day of that month, all the youths who had begun to be armed as warriors, each [with] their fathers and relatives, arrived at the Haucaypata plaza of Cuzco. It should be noted that everyone who was being armed, or was to be armed as a warrior, was and had to be high-status individuals, who were descendants and relatives of the Inca Lords through [a] direct male line, because no one else was allowed [to participate]. Also in this same month, wherever they might be, the governors appointed by the Inca who belonged to his lineage, if they had sons [coming] of age, would perform the same ceremonies in their provinces, [and] pierce their [sons'] ears and arm them as warriors.[144]

And on this day they would bring the *huacas* of the Creator, Sun, Thunder, and Moon to the plaza and place them all beside the Inca. The priests of the Creator, Sun, Moon, and Thunder, each of which was with his *huaca* at that time, would give those who had been armed as warriors certain clothes called *vmisca onco* [multi-colored tunic], which was a tunic with red and white bands, a white mantle with a blue cord and a red tassel.[145] Everyone in this land had to make these clothes as tribute. Their relatives give them *ojotas* [sandals] made of a straw, called *cuya* [grass], which they considered valuable. And the priest of the Sun, who was the one who gave them the clothes in the name of the Sun, would order all the maidens to be brought before him and each of them to be given a dress, which included a red and white *axo* [skirt], called *angallo* [clothing for females], and a *lliclla* [mantle] of the same [colors] and a [blank space], which was like an open-ended bag of the same colors. These clothes [were] also part of those given [as] tribute to the Sun.

That concluded, they would prepare some poles that had a knife like an axe on the top (Figure 5.9).[146] They were of palm [wood and] were called *yauri* [staff] in their language. They hung from them some *guaracas* [blank space] called *guaraca[s]* [sling(s)] [made] of sinews and red wool with a bit of *chaguar* [maguey]. And thus, holding them straight like a pike, each of the [young men] would go in order to worship the *huacas* of the Creator, Sun, Moon, and Thunder and give obeisance to the Inca. Before this, their uncles

FIGURE 5.9
The bronze head of an Inca yauri. (Field Museum, catalog number 894.100388.
Photograph by Brian S. Bauer.)

and [other] relatives would have flogged them on their arms and legs and told them to be always brave and to take great care to serve the *huacas* and the Inca.

That concluded, they would leave the plaza in their groups, each one with those of his lineage, and they would go to sleep at an uninhabited [place] called Rauraua,[147] which might be about one league from Cuzco (Map 5.3). Each one of those who had been armed as warriors took a tent in which he and those of his lineage would sleep. All the maidens who had received all the clothing that the Sun gave them would go with them. They called them *ñusta callixapa* [health princess]. They carried some small jugs of *chicha* to give the next day to drink to the relatives of the warriors, the youths who were armed as warriors, and for the sacrifice that was to be made.[148] This day they would take with them the ram called *topaguanaco* [splendid guanaco], and by another name, *raymi napa* [ritual sacred llama], which had a kind of red cloth tunic over it [and] gold ear [tassels], as has already been mentioned. They also took the *suntur paucar* [royal banner], [and together] these were the royal insignias. After the people left the plaza, they would take each of the *huacas* to its temple and the Inca would go to his house.

They would rise the next day in the morning and reach the ravine of a hill called Quilliya Colca,[149] which was a little more than half a league from where they had slept, and there they ate. On finishing, they tied a bit of white wool on the top of the poles that they carried in their hands, and on the head of the *topa yauri* [splendid staff], [they tied] a bit of *ychu* [a native grass]. In this way, they would walk until they reached a hill called Anaguarque, which might be two leagues from Cuzco, in order to give offerings to the *huaca* of the same name, on the top of that hill.[150] It was [a] *huaca* of the Indians

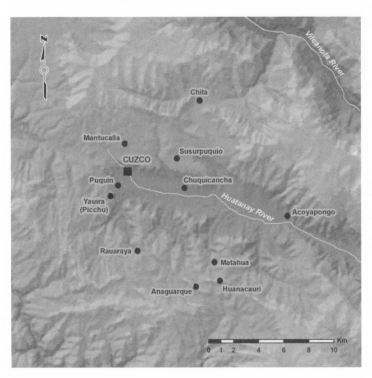

MAP 5.3
Selected locations in the Cuzco Basin mentioned by Molina.

of the towns of Choco and Caciona.[151] The reason they went to this *huaca* to make this sacrifice was because that day they would run a race to see who was the fastest. That is why they held this ceremony, because they say that at the time of the Flood this *huaca* remained so agile that it ran as fast as a hawk flew.

Having arrived there, the youths would offer that *huaca* a bit of wool that they carried in their hands. The priests of the Sun, [but] not the High [Priest], and those of the other *huacas* already mentioned, called *tarpuntaes*, would sacrifice five lambs, burning them to the Creator, Sun, Thunder, Moon, and the Inca, one to each of them, saying the already-mentioned phrases. The relatives would once again flog the young men [who were] now warriors with the mentioned *guaracas* [slings], telling them to always remember their own valor and bravery.

That finished, the people would settle down and perform the *taqui* called *guarita* with the *guayliaquipas* [shell trumpets] and shells mentioned above. While they were performing it, the warriors remained standing, holding the *yauri* [staff] poles in their hands, which were the weapons that they were given. Some of their [blank space] that were on the poles were made of gold and others of copper, each according to their means.

On finishing that *taqui*, all the maidens, called *ñusta calejapa* [health princess], would stand up and each one would run as fast as she could until reaching the Auraba,[152] where they had slept the night before. There they waited with the *chicha* to give to those who had been armed as warriors to drink, crying out [and] saying, "Come quickly, valiant youths! We are waiting here!" And then all those young warriors stood up, each in a row according to their order before the *huaca* of Anaguarque, evenly spaced, and another arrangement of men set up in a row in order behind them. These served as standard-bearers; they carried the already mentioned *yauris* [staffs] and poles in their hands. Then another arrangement of men stood up, each and everyone, in a row, [blank space] who were to help in case [anyone] fainted. And in front of everyone, [blank space] a splendidly dressed Indian. He would shout out, and on hearing this, all [the youths] would begin to run as fast as they could with utmost speed. In this way, if they fell or fainted, they helped each other, [but] some of them broke [their] shins and others died from the falls.[153] Having arrived at where the maidens were [waiting] with the *chicha*, [the maidens] gave to drink [blank space] and to the youths armed as warriors who came running in this way. The reason for this race was to learn who was the fastest of all those who were armed as warriors, [and] more than eight hundred youths were armed each time.[154] Once everyone was together on the hill called Yauraba,[155] they would all again perform that *taqui* called *guari*. On finishing that, they would take the *guaracas* [slings] from the *yauris* [staffs] and again flog the warriors on their arms and legs. When that concluded, probably already the hour of vespers, everyone rose according to their order to return to Cuzco in their order, carrying in front of them as royal insignias the *suntur paucar* [royal banner] and the ram called *raymi napa* [ritual sacred llama].

Thus they arrived according to their order at the Cuzco plaza called Haucaypata, where the figures or statues of the Creator, Sun, Thunder, and Moon had been [placed]. The Inca sat next to the statue of the Sun with those of his court, and as they entered in order [they] performed the *mucha* [veneration] to the Creator, Sun, [the] other *huacas*, and to the Inca. The [H]anan Cuzco and the Hurin Cuzco groups each sat on their own sides [while] the youths who had been armed as warriors remained standing. For a brief while, they would perform again the *taqui* called *guari*, during which they would again flog those youths in the same aforementioned order. The same was done, and in the same order, for those who were to succeed the Inca and Lord. [When] it was time to leave, the Inca went with the courtiers to his house and the armed warriors went with their fathers and relatives to the hill called Yauira.

That night they would sleep at the foot of the hill in a place called Guamancancha.[156] In the morning at sunrise, they would rise and climb the hill called Yauira, which, as mentioned, is half a league from Cuzco.[157] On this day the Lord Inca would go there to do more [activities] with those who had been armed as warriors, giving them gold earrings, red mantles with blue tassels, and other things out of generosity.

The Yauira *huaca* consisted of two stone hawks placed on an altar on top of the hill. Pachacuti Inca Yupanqui established this *huaca* so that [the warriors] would go there to receive their short trousers or loincloths, which they call *guara*. This *huaca* belonged originally to the Maras Indians, and Huascar Inca ordered the hawks to be placed [at] the *huaca* to embellish [it]. The sacrifice that was made to it was the burning of five lambs and the pouring of *chicha*, [while] pleading with the Creator, Sun, Thunder, and Moon to make those who were being armed as warriors valiant and fortunate fighters, to grant them good fortune in all that they did, and for [them] [to] never be defeated. The sacrifice was offered by the priest of the Yauira *huaca*, pleading with the *huaca* to give the youths good fortune. And once the sacrifice was burned, the *huaca[ca]mayo* [shrine specialist], who was the priest, would give each of the youths loincloths that they call *guara* and red tunics with white stripes. This clothing was brought by order of the Inca from the tribute that was made across the land for this purpose. He would [also] give them gold earplugs, which they would fasten there in their ears; diadems of feathers that they call *pilco cassa* [*pilco* feather diadem]; and medallions of silver and others of gold, similar to and of the size of plates, which were hung from the neck to embellish them.[158] Once they received these, they would eat and then perform the *taqui* called *guari*, which lasted for the space of one hour. That finished, the uncles and relatives again flogged the armed warriors, saying to them the mentioned prayers and telling them to emulate their ancestors, to be valiant warriors, [and] to never retreat.[159]

They say that this *taqui*, which they repeated so many times in this festival, was given by the Creator at the time when Manco Capac, their first Inca [and the one] from whom everyone descends, emerged from the cave of Tambo[toco], so that they would sing it in this festival and in no other. After they finished the *taqui*, they left according to their order, walking to Cuzco, carrying the *suntur paucar* [royal banner] in front, like a flag or banner, and the ram, dressed as has been described. As we already mentioned in the *History of the Incas*, Manco Capac instituted this festival [and] made his son Sinchi Roca undergo the ceremonies.[160] Thus, when they arrived at the plaza of Cuzco, they performed the *mocha* [veneration] and worshipped the *huacas* mentioned before, which their priests had already brought to the plaza. Following their order, each also made obeisance to all the embalmed bodies of the dead lords and ladies. Those who were in charge of the [bodies] had brought them to the plaza to drink with them as if they were alive, and so that those who had been armed as warriors could beseech the bodies, to make them as fortunate and brave as they had been.

That concluded, everyone would sit according to their groups. Those of [H]anan Cuzco and Hurin Cuzco already had some lion skins prepared with the heads still attached.[161] [The lions] had gold earrings in their ears and gold disks on their heads. They put gold teeth in place of the [real] teeth, which they had removed, and [they placed] gold bracelets on the paws, which they call *chipana* [thin metal]. They called these lions *hillacunya* [sacred neck?] [and] *chuquecunya* [gold neck]. They put them on their [own] heads so that all the [animal's] neck and head rose above the ones who were wearing them and [so that] the body of the lion draped over their back. Those who were to take part in the *taqui* wore red tunics reaching their feet, with white and red fringes. They called these tunics *puca caycho anco* [red, unknown term, tunic]. This *taqui*, [called] *coyo* [*sic*; *cayo*],[162] was invented by Pachacuti Inca Yupanqui and it was performed with drums, two from [H]anan Cuzco and two from Hurin Cuzco.[163] They performed this *taqui* twice a day and on finishing it, they performed the *taqui* [called] *guallina* [chant]. This way of dancing lasted six days and in each of those six days they made sacrifices for the Creator, Sun, Moon, Thunder, Inca, and for those who had been armed as warriors. The sacrifice they performed [involved] a great quantity of livestock, clothes, gold, silver, and other things. They performed the sacrifice so that those who were armed as warriors would be fortunate in war and in everything else they would undertake.

FIGURE 5.10

There are several known examples of the uauaclla tunics described by Molina.
(Tunic. Peru, Inca, ca. 1400–1540. Tapestry; cotton and camelid fiber; 84.1 x 76.2 cm.
The Cleveland Museum of Art. Gift of William R. Carlisle 1957.136.)

On the twenty-first day of the month, all those who had been armed as warriors would go to bathe in a spring called Calix Puquio, which is about a quarter of a league behind the fortress of Cuzco.[164] There they removed the clothing in which they had been armed as warriors and they dressed [in] others, which were called *uauaclla*, [which] were black and yellow with a red cross in the middle (Figure 5.10).

From there they returned to the plaza where they found all the *huacas* mentioned before, and [having] made their accustomed obeisance, they joined their respective groups where each one's relatives stood. The most principal uncle would give them a shield, a sling, and a club, so that they could have [weapons] to go to war. Later, the other relatives and *caciques* [local lords] would give them clothes, livestock, gold, silver, and other different things [so that] they would always be wealthy and without needs. Each of the [relatives] who gave [a gift] would [also] flog him once and lecture him, telling him to be valiant, to never be a traitor to the Sun or the Inca, to always remember the rituals of the *huacas*, and to emulate his ancestors in their valor and bravery.[165] And when the Inca, [the] principal lord, was armed as a warrior, all the paramount *caciques* [local lords] and lords from all the land who were there would give him great offerings. Besides the above-mentioned [things], they would give him shepherds for the livestock that they would give him. On finishing that, the priests of the Sun and Creator would bring many bundles of firewood. The bundles, dressed with men's and women's clothes, were offered dressed in that way to the Creator, Sun, and [the] Inca. They burned them in those clothes along with a ram.[166] They also burned some birds called *pilco pechio* [*pilco* bird] and *camantera pechio* [*camantera* bird]. This sacrifice was done for those who had been armed as warriors, praying to the Creator and the Sun to always make them fortunate in warfare.

On the twenty-second day of the month, they would take [some of] the warriors to the *chacras* [fields] and others to their houses, and they would pierce their ears.[167] This was the last ceremony that they performed in arming them as warriors. The ear piercing was of such [blank space] among these nations that if an [earlobe] broke on piercing, from the piercing onward they were seen as unlucky.[168] They put some cotton and wool threads, wrapped in cotton, into the holes of the ears. And each day they put in larger [ones] so that the hole in the ear would become larger.[169] That concluded, on the same day, the priests of the Creator, Sun, Thunder, and Moon, and the shepherds of the Inca would occupy themselves in counting the livestock of the *huacas* and [the] Inca. That day the celebrations would begin that they performed for the livestock, [and they would make offerings to] the Creator, Sun, Thunder, and Moon so that the livestock would multiply.[170] They performed this sacrifice for the livestock on the same day across the entire kingdom [blank space] [when] they sprayed the livestock with *chicha*.[171] They [also] gave clothing and food to the shepherds of the livestock. The one whose cattle had increased the most received a better payment and, consequently, the one [blank space] they punished.

On the twenty-third day of the month, they would take the statue of the Sun, called Huayna Punchao, to the Houses of the Sun called Puquin. They are on a tall hill a little more than three harquebus shots from Cuzco,[172] and there they made sacrifices. They made sacrifices to the Creator, Sun, Thunder, and Moon, on behalf of all the nations, so that the people would multiply and all the households [would] prosper. They occupied themselves these days drinking and resting. On finishing, they returned the statue of the Sun, carrying in front of it the *suntur paucar* [royal banner] and two rams, one of gold and the other of silver, called *collquenapa* [silver sacred llama] [and] *corinapa* [gold sacred llama]. [They did so] since these were the insignias that the statue of the Sun carried wherever it went. And in this way the holy period and month called Capac Raymi ended.

DECEMBER

They called the month of December Camay Quilla.[173] On the first day of the moon, those who had been armed as warriors, from the [H]anan Cuzco [Upper Cuzco] group as well as Hurin Cuzco [Lower Cuzco], would arrive at the plaza with slings called *guaracas* [slings] in their hands. Those of [H]anan Cuzco and Hurin Cuzco would hurl shots to [hit] each other with a [blank space] that they call *coco*,[174] which grows on some cacti, and on some occasions they came to blows to test their strength until the Inca, who was already in the plaza, stood up and called for peace. They called this [fighting] *chocanaco* [stoning]. They did this in order to learn who were the strongest and the bravest.

When finished, everyone sat according to their groups, [with] the new warriors wearing new clothes: black tunics, small tan mantles, and white feathers on their heads from birds they call *tocto*.[175] And so, they would begin to eat. This day they would eat salt and [all] the other foods, because they always fasted and did not eat salt or chili when they were armed as warriors.[176] So the youths, who in that way had been armed as warriors, ate with much joy because their fast had ended.

To perform this festival, they would bring to the plaza all the mentioned *huacas* and the bodies of the deceased Inca kings and queens to drink with them, placing those who had been lords of [H]anan Cuzco within that group and those of Hurin Cuzco within their group. They brought food and drink to the dead as if they were alive, saying: "When you were alive, you used to eat and drink this. [May] your soul receive and eat it now, wherever [your soul] may be."[177] [They said this] because they believed, and were very sure, that the souls did not die and that those of good [people] went to rest with the Creator. That was what they said when they died, entrusting their relatives, their households, and families. [They] said that if the [living] performed and fulfilled what the [deceased] request[ed], they would see them again from heaven. They [also] believed that there was a hell for evil [people] and that there the demons, which they call *cupay* [demon], tormented them. They said that those who went to hell suffered great hunger and thirst, and that the foods they ate and drank were coal, snakes, toads, and other foods of this type. Those who went to heaven would eat and drink with great splendor the very fine foods that the Creator had arranged for them. Also, they would receive the foods and drinks that were burned for them here [on earth].[178]

And thus, everyone spent this day with great satisfaction and joy as they began the song and dance [called] *yabayra* that lasted two days, following the same order. When finished, they all left to plow their *chacras* [fields], calling the plow *chacma* in their language. This lasted twelve days, and with the previous two, made fourteen. On the fifteenth day, during the full moon, everyone had to return from

their farms [blank spaced] to Cuzco.[179] That night they would occupy themselves performing the dance and *taqui* called *yaguayra*
along all the streets and blocks of Cuzco, from dusk until dawn. In
the morning, those who were in charge of [them] would bring the
huacas of the Creator, Sun, Thunder, Moon, and the dead bodies [of
the Inca royalty] to the plaza, where they would set them in their
places. The Inca would [then] arrive to take his [place], because
[this] was next to the Sun.

By this time, everyone else had gone to a house that they called
Moro Vrco, which was next to the Houses of the Sun, to take out a
very long rope that they kept there. [It was] made of four colors:
black, white, red, and tan.[180] At the beginning of [the rope], it had
a ball of thick red wool. They would all take hold of it with both
hands, the men on one part and the women on another, performing
the *taqui* called *yaguayra*. [As] those in front arrived at the plaza,
they made obeisance to the *huacas* and then to the Inca, still holding
the *guasca* [sacred rope].[181] And so, the [rest] did the same as they
were entering [the plaza]. They circled around the entire plaza and
once the extremes [of the rope] were joined, the beginning with the
end, they performed their *taqui* in their order in such a way that,
when they finished, [the rope] looked like a snail. And they would
drop the *guasca* [sacred rope] to the ground, leaving it coiled like a
snake. Because it was shaped like a snake, they called this rope Moro
Orco.

[Then] they would go to sit in their seats and those who were
in charge of the *guasca* would take it to its house. They performed
these celebrations with clothes that they call *pucay onco*, which were
black shirts with a white band along the bottom, white fringes on its
edges, and the feathers were white from some birds called *tocto*. After this, they would offer a lamb to be sacrificed to the rope, the rain,
and the wintertime, while asking the winter, "Why has it rained?"

They spent this day resting and drinking with the Sun, the other
huacas, and [the] dead bodies [of the rulers] until a half hour before
sunset. And because I [already] mentioned in the Inti Raymi, which
is in the month of May, the way that they had of drinking with the

Sun and the other *huacas,* which, as I noted, [involved] pouring the *chicha* in certain wells, I will not mention it here. In all the celebrations, the drinking with the *huacas* was [done] in the same way. And as I say, half an hour before sunset, they would take the *huacas* to their houses and the Inca would go to his own. Performing this *taqui,* sacrifice, and drinking would last for two days.

On the eighteenth day of the month, they arrived at the plaza dressed in very elegant clothes called *angas onco* [blue tunic], *quilapi onco* [silvery tunic], and small mantles, and on their heads [they wore] feathers called *cupa ticas* [tail feathers], which are from [the] tails of *guacamayas* [macaws] and *pilco[s].* [These headdresses were] called *gualanbabi* [large plumage] and were made of feathers. [Having] arrived at the plaza, they made their obeisance to the *huacas* in the order already mentioned. Once they were in their places, a priest would stand up and burn a lamb in sacrifice, beseeching the winter to always send its waters, by which they could eat and drink. They saved the charcoal and ashes from this sacrifice, as well as those from all the others that they made during the year, to throw them into the river the following day, as will be described. On this day they performed the *taqui* [called] *chapayguanlo* [tail song], which, like all the other ceremonies that were carried out during the entire year, was invented by Pachacuti Inca Yupanqui Cupa.[182] The *guarachico* [male initiation rite], which is when they arm warriors, and those of the *quicochico* [female initiation rite], *rutuchico* [first hair-cutting rite], and *ayascay* [birth rite], which are the celebrations that the first Inca invented, will be mentioned in their place, explaining their names.

The next day, which was the nineteenth day of the month, the Inca and all the other people would go to the plaza of Cuzco, called, as has been described, Haucaypata. They also brought [there] all the other *huacas* and the embalmed bodies of the dead, where [after] having paid the accustomed obeisances, they began to perform the sacrifice called *maiucati,* in the following way.

A small river passes through Cuzco, called Capi Mayo[183] and [also] Guacapanco Maio, which descends down from some ravines that are above Cuzco. Even though it was winter, they would build some rows of dams [in the river] to collect water so that the offerings that were to be thrown into it could be carried off with greater force. For this day they would have prepared all kinds and sorts of food that they used: all the types of chilies, a large number of coca baskets, all the [different] kinds of colored clothes that they wore and [the] shoes that they used; [the] *llautos* [headbands] and feathers that they placed on their head, [as well as] livestock, flowers, gold, silver, and everything that they used; also everything else and the charcoals that they had saved from the sacrifices that they had performed during the entire year. They would throw all of this into the river and on breaking the first dam, the [water] would cascade down with such force that it would break the other [dams] and carry the sacrifices away.

[On] this day a lamb was burned in sacrifice, throwing its ashes and the charcoal, along with everything else, into the river (Map 5.4). Many people would stand on either side [of the river] at the outskirts of the city of Cuzco in a place that they call Pomapi Chupa,[184] where they used to cast all those sacrifices. They would throw them in a little less than an hour before the sun set. The Lord Inca, who was present, would order the Indians who were on either side of the river throwing the sacrifices into the river to follow the sacrifice to Ollantaytambo, which, with the detour that they took, might be ten leagues from Cuzco. All the way to that town [alongside the river] were Indians from the towns through which [the sacrifice] had to pass, stationed in places with straw torches in order to burn during the night, making sure that nothing of the sacrifice was left in the river [and] giving light to those who were following [the offerings]. Once the sacrifices reached the Ollantaytambo bridge, which is a large river that goes to the Northern Sea,[185] they would throw from the bridge two baskets of coca, called *pilco longo* [and] *paucar ongo* [*pilco* basket and multicolored basket]. And with this, they allowed the sacrifices to go on their own. That day and the next, those who had followed [the sacrifices] drank, rested, and performed the *taqui* [called] *chupay guayllo* [tail song].[186]

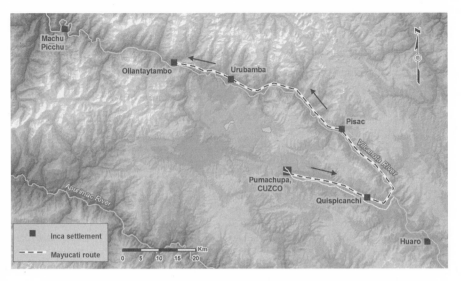

MAP 5.4

The course of the offerings as they floated between Cuzco and Ollantaytambo.

They say that the reason they threw these sacrifices into the river was so that the Creator of All Things, who had given them a very prosperous year, would deem it proper to give them another good [year]. [They also say that] they performed the offering[s] and sacrifice[s] with the things that he had given them so that he would not see them as ingrates, asking him to openly receive [the offerings], wherever he might be. And if by chance he was in the sea, which they call *mamacocha*, [they ask him] to receive it wherever he was. For this reason, they threw the sacrifices into the river, saying it would take them to the sea.

At the end of two days, those who had followed the sacrifice to the bridge returned to Cuzco. Those who had run the fastest carried a spear made of salt in their hands, and others, hawks of salt. The last ones, those who had run the slowest, [carried] some toads of salt, so that it would be known how slowly they had run and how little they amounted to. This was grounds for mocking them and for some amusement. During the remainder of the month, everyone would work on their estates.

THE MONTH OF JANUARY

They called the month of January Atun Pucuy. They had no particular celebration in it; they were only occupied in their tasks.

FEBRUARY

They called the month of February Pacha Pucu. They also did nothing more than improve the *chacras* [fields].

MARCH

They called the month of March Paucar Guara. They also did not have any festival in it.

APRIL

They called the month of April Ayriguay.[187] They harvested the *chacras* in it and they also gathered and stored [the harvest], calling this [practice] *aymoray* (Figure 5.11). Those who had been armed as warriors would go to the *chacra* [field] of Sausiro to collect the maize that had been harvested in it. [This field] is below the arch where they say that Mama Huaco, sister of Manco Capac, the first Inca, planted the first maize.[188] Each year they cultivated this *chacra* [field] for the body of Mama Huaco, making from it [the] *chicha* that was needed for the [ser]vice of that body. Thus the [warriors] carried [the maize] in and deliver[ed] it to the people who were in charge of that body, which was embalmed. They then successively gathered the maize from the *chacras* [fields] of the Creator, Sun, Moon, Thunder, Inca, Huanacauri, and of all the dead kings.[189] Wearing some handsome clothes, they carried it in some small sacks, [singing] a song called *araui*.[190] And all the other people of Cuzco would go to gather the maize, except on the first day [when] the youths armed as warriors would bring it. The priests, called

FIGURE 5.11

Like all agriculturists, the Incas held celebrations to mark the time of harvest. Guaman Poma de Ayala depicts the maize harvest here. The caption reads "May Great Harvest Month." Near the bottom of the page is written "They carry food to the storehouses." (Drawing by Guaman Poma de Ayala [1980 (1615): 244 (246)].) (Courtesy of Det Kongelige Bibliotek.)

tarpuntaes, would [also] burn a lamb in sacrifice, asking the Creator to always grant good years. This would last four days [and] when finished, they would all go to their estates. And thus the year ended in this way and the month of May returned, beginning [with] the festival of the Sun.

Chapter 6

THE *AYUSCAY, RUTUCHICO,* AND *QUICOCHICO* RITUALS

*B*esides the ceremonies that they hold during these months, they performed others, as we have mentioned, called *apuscay* [birth celebration], *rotuchico* [first hair-cutting rite], [and] *ticochico* [female initiation rite]. Although in these no ... [*sic*] ... so that the traditions that these people had can be understood.[1] The *ayuscay* [birth celebration] [was held] on the fourth day after a woman gave birth. On this day they placed the infant in a cradle, which they called *quirao* [cradle], and they summoned the uncles and relatives so that they could see the infant. On arriving, they drank that day, though they did not carry out any other ceremony.[2]

The *rutuchico* [first hair-cutting rite] is when an infant, be it a male or a female, turns one year [and] they gave it the name that it was to have until it came of age. If it was a male, [this was] when he was armed as a warrior and was given a *guaraca* [sling]. This is when they were given the names that they kept until death. If it was a female, she received the name that she was to keep forever at the time of her first menstruation. Thus, on its first birthday, they sheared the infant's hair.[3] To do the shearing, they asked the closest uncle to be the first to cut the infant's hair, and he would present [an offering] to the child. This was repeated until [all] the relatives made the[ir] offering[s] and then the parents' friends would do it. [On] this day, they would drink, and the principal uncle would give [the infant] the name that it was to have until it came of age, as was mentioned above.[4]

The *quicochico* [female initiation rite] is when a woman has her

75

first menstruation. [This celebration] lasted about three days, from the first day that [the menstruation] began until it was finished. The first two days they fasted, without eating anything. The next day they gave her a bit of uncooked maize, telling [her] not to die of hunger, and she rested quietly in a place within her house. On the fourth day, she would bathe and put on clothes called *angallo axo* [a female skirt] and *ojotas* [sandals] of white wool. They would do her hair and place a *toca* [unknown term] on her head that was shaped like a bag. This day, her most principal [relative] and the rest [of her] relatives would arrive, and she would come out to serve them food and to give them beverages. This lasted two days. Her most principal relative [then] would give her the name that she was to have [thenceforth], and would warn and counsel her on how she was to live and obey her parents. This they called *coñanaco* [unknown term]. They also gave her what they could, according to their means, and all the other relatives and friends gave her the fine items she would need for a household. And this was done without any particular idolatry, being established in this form by Inca Yupanqui.[5]

When the Inca gave wives to them, which they received, the man would go to the house of the young woman's father to tell him that the Inca had given her to him, and that although [this] was ordered by the Inca, [the man] wanted to serve him. And thus the relatives [blank space] of her would gather and try to earn each other's goodwill. And [then] the young man would go to his father-in-law and mother-in-law's house for a period of four or five days, bringing them straw and firewood. In this way an agreement was reached. [So] he would take her as wife because the Inca, who was giving her to him, told [the young man] that he was giving her to him until death. And with that condition he received her, and there was no one who dared to leave her.[6]

Chapter 7

THE CAPACOCHA

*P*achacuti Inca Yupanqui also invented the Capacocha, which was [carried out] in the following way. The provinces of Collasuyo, Chinchaysuyo, Antisuyo, and Cuntisuyo would bring to this city, from each town and lineage of people, one or two small boys or girls, of ten years old.[1] They would also bring clothes and livestock, as well as sheep [made] of gold, silver, and *mullu*. These were kept in Cuzco for the reasons that will be told. After all this was assembled, the Inca would sit in the plaza of Haucaypata, which is the large plaza of Cuzco. There the children and other sacrifices walked around the statues of the Creator, Sun, Thunder, and Moon that were already in the plaza for this purpose. They made two turns [around them], and after finishing, the Inca summoned the provincial priests and had the offerings divided into four parts for the four suyos: Collasuyo, Chinchaysuyo, Antisuyo, and Cuntisuyo, which are the four regions into which this land is divided. And he would tell them, "Each of you take your share of these offerings and sacrifices, take it to your principal *huaca*, and sacrifice them there." And [having] taken them, [the priests] would carry them to the *huaca* and there they would suffocate the children and bury them together with the silver sheep and gold and silver human figurines.[2] [Also] they would burn the sheep, rams, and clothes, as well as small baskets of coca. The people of Cuzco would take the mentioned sacrifices to Sacalpiña,[3] which is about one league from Cuzco, where the Indians of Anta would receive them. And so they delivered them to where the sacrifices were to be made, and continuing in this way, they would take [the offerings] to the rest of the provinces.

They conducted this sacrifice at the beginning of the Lord Inca's rule so that the *huacas* would grant him good health, keep his kingdoms and dominions in peace and serenity, [allow him] to reach old age, and to live without illness. In this way, no *huaca*, or *mochadero*[4] [place of worship], or shrine, no matter how small it could be, ever lacked [a share of the] sacrifice, because it had already been determined and decided what was to be sacrificed at each *huaca*, place, and location.

The reason [the] parts of the sacrifice had to be enough for all the *huacas*, shrines, trees, springs, hills, [and] lakes was that they portended that none [of the *huacas*] should be missed, so that none of them would become angry and furiously punish the Inca due to a lack of an offering.[5] If they arrived at some high hills that they could not climb because of the rough [terrain], they would throw the sacrifice with slings from [where] they were able to [reach]. Thus, the above-mentioned sacrifice and offering were made at all the principal *huacas* in all the provinces. They went first to them and then [to] all the *huaquillos*[6] [little shrines] and shrines that were in the whole province, giving each one what had been set aside for it in Cuzco, since in Cuzco [there] was its *quipocamayo* [record keeper], who is like [a] record keeper for each of the shares, who kept track of and calculated the sacrifices that were to be made in each province.

They would begin making the sacrifices in the city of Cuzco in the following way. The first sacrifice [was] to the Creator.[7] The priests who were in charge of his statue received the sacrifice, pleading with him to deem it proper to give the Inca long life, health, victory against his enemies, and not to take him in his youth, or his sons, or descendants. [They also pleaded] that while this Inca was Lord all the nations he kept subjugated would always be in peace, multiply, have food, and that [he] would always be victorious. Having made this prayer, they suffocated the children, having first provided food and drink to those who were old enough, while their mothers [blank space] to the little ones, saying that [in this way] they would not arrive hungry or unhappy where the Creator was. Other [children] had their live hearts taken out, and so the priests offered the beating [hearts] to the *huacas* to which the sacrifice was made.[8] They also spread the blood almost from ear to ear [across] the face of the *huaca*,[9] and they called this [ritual] *pirac*. Other [*huacas*] were given the body with that blood, and in this way, they buried the bodies, along with all the other sacrifices, in a place called Chuquicancha.[10] As has been mentioned, this is a small hill above San Sebastián, which must be half a league from Cuzco.[11] Then, continuing in the ~~manner~~ same manner, the priests of the Sun received those [sacrifices] that were [to be] dedicated to the Sun, and in that same place, they carried out the sacrifice to the Sun with the following prayer:

*Viracochaya punchao cachan tota cachan nispac nic pacarichon
yllarichon nispac nic punchae churiyquicta carillaclla quispillacta
puricho runa rurascayquicta cancharin gampac quillarin ganpac
uiracochaya.*

*Casilla quispilla punchao ynga runa yana nichiscayquicta qui-
llari canchari ama oncochispa ama nanachispa caçista quispicta
huacaychaspa.*

Translation:

O Creator, [you] who gave [blank space] and [you] who said [let there] be night and day, sunrise and sunlight, tell your son the Sun that when it is dawn to emerge in peace. Keep him safe so that he may shine on the men that you created. O Creator!

O Sun. [You] who are safe and in peace, shine on these people that you watch over. Guard them from sickness. Keep them safe and sound.[12]

In this same way, [they offered] to the Thunder, which they call

Chuqueylla. The priests who were in charge of its statue, the shape of which has already been described,[13] would receive the infants and the other sacrifices that were dedicated for this [purpose], and they would bury them in the same way, in the place already mentioned called Chuquicancha. They [also] used to bury the sacrifices for the Moon in the same way and in the same place, pleading with her to always keep the Inca healthy and prosperous, and [for him] to always defeat his enemies. Then all the priests together offered to the heavens the part of the sacrifice that was reserved for that, and also to the earth, reciting the following prayer:

> *Pachamama cuyru mama casillacta quispellacta capac ynga gua-*
> *guayyquicta macari hatalli.*
>
> *O Mother Earth! Hold the Inca, your son, always on top of you,*
> *calm and peaceful.*

All the described sacrifices were brought to that place. Then the priest who was in charge of the *huaca* of Huanacauri, where they claim [that] Ayarcache, one of the four brothers who they say emerged from the cave of [Pacari]Tambo, was turned into stone, [received the sacrifices]. Because this [myth] was included and discussed at length in the fable at the beginning of the *History [of the Incas]*, which Your Most Illustrious Majesty has, I do not discuss it here. Your Most Illustrious Lordship can read it there.[14] Thus, as [Huanacauri] was the most important *huaca* that they had, besides the ones already mentioned, and being such, the priest who was in charge of it, with the rest of his companions, would receive the infants and things that were dedicated [to the shrine]. And they would sacrifice and bury [the offerings] on that hill called Huanacauri, which is two and a half leagues from Cuzco, more or less. At the time of the offering, while the sacrifice was burning, they would say a prayer, pleading [for] the Inca, his descendant, to always be youthful, always be victorious, and never be defeated; that while this Inca was Lord, everything should be always at peace. Then, they would cast into all the places, springs, and hills that were [held] in Cuzco as shrines the sacrifices that were dedicated for them, [but] without killing any infants for these [sacrifices]. There were so many places in Cuzco that were dedicated for sacrifices that it would be very tedious if I describe them here. And because all the ways they sacrificed [at them] are included in the *Account of the Huacas* that I gave to Your Most Illustrious Majesty, I will not include this [information] here.[15]

Having finished with what was to be sacrificed in Cuzco, the priests brought out the sacrifices that were to be taken [to other regions], as has already been mentioned.[16] The way they approached [the *huacas*] with the sacrifices was [the following]: All the people that [went] with the Capacocha, which by another name is called Cachaguaes,[17] went grouped in bands, somewhat separated from one another. [They] did not go directly by the royal road, but [in contrast, they would go] without turning anywhere,[18] traversing the gorges and mountains that they found before them, until each one reached the part and place that [blank place] were waiting to receive the aforementioned sacrifices. They would walk [and,] at intervals, led by one Indian who had been especially chosen and taught for this purpose, they would raise their voices and shout. As he began, everyone followed him with these shouts. In these they asked the Creator [for] the Inca to always be victorious, never be defeated, and to always live in safety and in peace. They carried on their shoulders [and] in front [of everyone], the gold and silver statues, the rams, and [the] other things that were to be sacrificed. The infants who could walk went on foot, [and] those who could not were carried by their mothers. The Inca, rams, and lambs would go by the royal road.

And thus, once they reached each part and place, those who were to perform the sacrifices, the *huacacamayos* [shrine specialists], which means "guardian of the *huacas*," and who were in charge of them, each received the sacrifice that corresponded to their *huaca*. They would sacrifice and offer [those items], burying the gold, silver, *mullu* sacrifices, and other things that they used. The infants who were assigned to [each] *huaca* were suffocated first. They [also] burned the rams, lambs, and clothes assigned to them. It should be noted that they did not sacrifice infants to all the *huacas*, but only to the main *huacas* held by the provinces or lineages.

Like this, they would continue walking across each of the four regions of the land that the Inca had conquered, making those sacrifices until each had arrived, following the route they were going, to the farthest borders and boundary markers that the Inca had established.[19] They had such [accurate] accounting and calculations about this [celebration], and [since] what was to be sacrificed in each area and place left Cuzco so well allotted, that although the sacrifice made was enormous and the places where it was to be done [were] innumerable, there was never an error nor did they mistake one place with another. For this purpose, the Inca had Indians from the four *suyos* or regions in Cuzco; each one [of them] had accounts and calculations of all the *huacas* of that region in which he was a *quipucamaio*, or record keeper, no matter how small [the *huaca*] might be. They called them *vilcacamaio* [shrine specialists], and [each] Indian was in charge of almost five hundred leagues of land. These had the accounts and calculations of the things that were to be sacrificed to each *huaca*, and so those who were to leave Cuzco took [the accounts] from the [*vilcacamayo*]. They would subsequently give the calculations and accounts to the ones who would deliver the offerings from one to another. Nevertheless, in the capitals of the provinces, there were also Indians delegated for this purpose, who had accounts and calculations of the sacrifices that were to remain in each province. But because they sometimes increased or reduced those sacrifices, according to the will of the Inca, they took from Cuzco the account of what was to be done in every part and place.

They held this sacrifice, called Capacocha or Cacha Guaco, in such veneration that if they were walking across an uninhabited [place], or anywhere, [and] they met some people, those who came upon the sacrifice [bearers] did not dare to raise [their] eyes and look at it.[20] Instead they prostrated [themselves] upon the ground until they passed. And in the inhabited towns that they reached, the inhabitants did not emerge from their houses, remaining [inside] with great reverence and humility until the Capacocha passed through and moved on.

What also occurred was that when they subjected and conquered other nations, they selected and took the most beautiful [people] that were among them, and took them to Cuzco, where they sacrificed them to the Sun for the victory that they said he had given them.

They also believed that if something excelled among all the others of its kind, because it was more beautiful, then they [should] worship it and make it a *huaca* and shrine. They worshipped all the mountain heights and summits, and offered more and other things [to them] because they said that when they climbed up a steep slope and reached its heights, they rested from their expended efforts there. This [worship] they called *chupasitas*.[21]

Chapter 8

TAQUI ONQOY

bout ten years ago,[1] more or less, a disaffection[2] began
to spread among the Indians of this land, during which
they performed a type of song that they called *taqui onqoy* [dance
sickness].[3] Because Luis de Olivera, a lay cleric in Parinacocha Province, which is in the bishopric of Cuzco, was the first to witness this
disaffection or idolatry while he was [the] priest of that territory,
he explains here about the manner in which they carried it out and
why.

In the province of Parinacocha of the bishopric of Cuzco, the
said Luis de Olivera, the vicar of that province, came to know that
not only in that province, but in all the other provinces and cities
of Chuquicaca, La Paz, Cuzco, La Paz, Cuzco [*sic*], Huamanga, and
even Lima and Arequipa, most of the [people] had fallen into great
apostasies. [They were] departing from the Catholic faith that they
had received and returning to the idolatry that they practiced in
[the] time of their infidelity. It could not be learned who could have
started this business, except it was suspected and discussed that it
was an invention of the sorcerers whom the Incas kept in Vilcabamba, where [the Incas] were uprising.[4] Because this is what was
believed to have occurred in this kingdom [blank space].

[In] the year of [15]70, and not before, the Indians held and believed that [people] had been sent from Spain to this kingdom [to
search] for an ointment of the Indians to cure a certain illness for
which no medicine was known except for that ointment.[5] In those
times [and] for this reason, the Indians went about very secretive-

ly, and [they] distanced themselves from the Spaniards to such a degree that no [Indian] wanted to take firewood, herb[s], or other things to a Spaniard's house. They say that [in this way, the Indian] would not be killed inside by having the ointment extracted from him.[6] All of this was believed to have originated in that robber's den [of Vilcabamba] to create enmity between the Indians and Spaniards.[7] As the Indians of this land held everything of the Inca in such high regard, and [as they] claimed that the [belief] originated there [in Vilcabamba], they were convinced very quickly in any [blank space] until the Lord Viceroy Don Francisco de Toledo defeated and expelled them from there, through which God Our Lord was greatly served.[8]

And returning to the resourcefulness of the devil in diverting these poor [souls],[9] [it happened] that they believed that all the *huacas* of the kingdom that the Christians had demolished and burned had come back to life, and had formed themselves into two sides: some had joined with the *huaca* of Pachacama[c] and the others with the *huaca* Titica[ca].[10] [They said] that all of them were flying around in the air, ordering [the people] to give battle to God and defeat Him. And [they claimed] that they were already defeating Him. [They said] that when the Marquis[11] entered this land, God had defeated the *huacas* and the Spaniards [had defeated] the Indians. But now, the world had turned around, [so] God and the Spaniards would be defeated this time, and all the Spaniards [would] die, their cities would be flooded, and the sea would rise and drown them so that no memory would be left of them. Within this apostasy, they believed that God, Our Lord, had made the Spaniards, Castile, and the animals and supplies of Castile, but that the *huacas* had made the Indians, this land, and the supplies that the Indians had before [the arrival of the Spaniards]. In this way, they were stripping Our Lord of his omnipotence.

Many preachers appeared from among the Indians, who preached both in the *punas* [high, remote grasslands] as well as in the settlements. They went about preaching this resurrection of the *huacas*, saying that the *huacas* now were flying through the air, dried out and dying of hunger, because the Indians no longer made sacrifices nor poured *chicha* to them. [The Indians said] that they had planted many *chacras* with worms to sow them in the hearts of the Spaniards, [in the] livestock of Castile and [in the] horses, and also in the hearts of the Indians who remained Christians. [They said] that [the *huacas*] were angry with all of the [Christian Indians] because they had been baptized and that [the *huacas*] would kill them all if they did not return to them, reneging on their Catholic faith. Those who wanted the friendship and grace [of the *huacas*] would live in prosperity, grace, and health. In order to return to [the *huacas*], they were to fast some days, not eat salt or chili, nor have sexual relations, nor eat colored maize, nor eat things of Castile, nor use them in food or in clothing, nor enter the churches, nor pray, nor respond to the calls of the priests, nor call themselves by Christian names. [They said] that in this way, they would return to the love of the *huacas* and they would not be killed. They also [preached] that the time of the Incas was returning and that the *huacas* [were] no longer entering stones, clouds, or springs to speak, but [they were] now themselves entering the Indians and making them speak. And that they should have their houses swept and prepared in case any *huaca* wanted to lodge there.

Accordingly, there were many Indians who trembled and threw themselves on the ground. Others threw stones as if possessed, grimacing, and then they rested. People would fearfully approach [the possessed person] and ask him what was happening and [what] he [was] experiencing, and he would answer that a certain *huaca* had entered his body. They would then take him in their arms and carry him to a special place, and there they would make a room with straw and blankets for him. Later, they would paint him in red[12] and the Indians would come in to worship him with rams, *colle* [dark purple] *chicha*, *llipta* [an ash mixture], *mullu*, and other things. And everyone would celebrate in the town for two or three days, dancing, drinking, and invoking the *huaca* that the [possessed person] represented and said was inhabiting his body. During the nights, [everyone] would stay awake without sleeping.

From time to time, these [possessed people] gave sermons to the town, extolling them not to serve God, [saying] that it was not the time of God but rather of *huacas,* and threatening the Indians if they did not completely abandon Christianity. They would argue with the *cacique,* or Indian who used a Christian rather than an Indian name, or [who] wore [a] shirt or [a] hat, or shoes, or any other item from Spain or Lusate.[13] These possessed ones would ask in the towns if there were any relics of the burned *huacas,* and when they [were] brought a piece of stone from them, they would cover their head with a blanket before the town, pour *chicha* over the stone, and rub it with white corn flour. Then they would shout, invoking the *huaca,* and later they would rise with the stone in their hands and tell the town, "Here you see your protection. And here you see the one who created you, and [who] gives you health, children, and *chacras.* Return it to its place, where it was during the time of the Incas." And thus the sorcerers who were secluded and punished in that [town] would carry this out with many sacrifices [blank space]. They freely used their ministries, returning to them, remaining beside the Indians that had become *huacas* and receiving the rams and *coies* [guinea pigs] for the sacrifices.

This evil was so widely believed and commonly celebrated that not only the Indians in the provinces[14] but [also] those who lived in the cities among Spaniards followed and believed in this wretchedness, fasting and corrupting [others]. During this period, no small number condemned themselves, because they died holding this belief. Finally, because the Vicar Luis de Olivera began to punish that province and that of Acarí, and he informed the Royal Audience of Lima, [the] archbishop and [the] bishop of the Charcas, [and] other parts, as well as Fray Pedro de Toro, administrator of the bishopric of Cuzco, [the movement] began to weaken. In all, it lasted more than seven years.

[The Indians] followed this apostasy [blank space] because they believed that God and the Spaniards were being defeated, [and] they tried to lead a revolt, as it was widely known in the year of [15]75 [*sic*].[15] [This was] when Licenciado Castro was the governor of these kingdoms.[16] He was informed of this from the chief magistrates of Cuzco, Huamanga,[17] and Huánuco [blank space] [that] these cities had taken up arms.[18]

During this time, there were different types of apostasies in different provinces. Some [Indians] danced, suggesting that the *huaca* was in their body. Others trembled for the same reason, suggesting that it was in them too. Others shut themselves up in their houses and shrieked. Others mutilated themselves, had fits, and killed [themselves]. Others jumped into rivers, offering themselves to the *huacas*. [This happened] until Our Lord was moved by his mercy to enlighten these miserable people. And those who continued [believing in the *huacas*], on seeing the Inca dead and Vilcabamba [in the hands] of Christians, now have realized the trickery that they believed and was preached to them. [These now believe] nothing of what occurred before, but [rather] the complete opposite.[19]

As a result of these demonic teachings, there are still some male and female Indian sorcerers, although not very many.[20] So when some male or female Indian is ill, they call the [sorcerer] to cure them and to tell them if the person will live or die. Having evaluated the situation, they order to be brought for the afflicted white maize, which they call *paracay cara* [white maize]; black[21] maize, which they call *colli cara* [dark purple maize]; mixed red and yellow maize, which they call *cuma cara*; [blank space] yellow [maize], which they call *paro çara* [dark yellow maize]; and other seashells that they call *mullu mullu* [many *Spondylus* shells], of every color there is, which they call *ymaymana mullu* [all kinds of *Spondylus* shells].[22] Having all this collected, the sorcerer requests [that] the maize and the *mullu* be ground together. Once [it is] ground, he places it in the afflicted hand so that he can blow it, offering it to the *huacas* and *uilcas* [holy places] of this land, saying these words:

> To all the *huacas* and *uilcas* of the four regions of this land, my grandfathers and ancestors, receive this sacrifice wherever you may be, and give me health.

They also make him blow a bit of coca to the Sun, offering it to him and asking him [for] good health. The same [was offered] to the Moon and the Stars. And then, that same afflicted person takes a little bit of gold and silver of little value in his hand, and pouring it, he offers it to the Creator.

After this, the sorcerer orders the afflicted person to feed his deceased [relatives]. If the [burials] are in a place where this can be done, then they place the food over the burials and pour *chicha* on them; if not, then [the offerings are made] in whatever part of the house the [sorcerer] believes [best]. [They do this] because the sorcerer makes [the afflicted person] believe that since [his ancestors] are starving to death, they have cast a curse upon him, causing him to be sick. And if by luck he is able to walk to the confluence of two rivers, [the sorcerer] makes him go there and wash his body with water and white maize flour, telling him to leave the illness there.[23] If not, then [it is done] in the afflicted person's house.

Once this is finished, [the sorcerer] talks with the afflicted person, telling him that if he wants to free himself of the illness, then he must confess to him all his sins, without omitting or hiding any. They call this *hichico* [confession].[24] And since these Indians are so gullible, there are some of them who easily, and with little persuasion, allow themselves to fall into this apostasy and error. Although later, with regret, some confess [to committing] this sin [along] with the others. There is also a very large number of male and female Indians who, because they already understand the offense that is done to Our Lord through this [apostasy], would not allow it at all, but rather reported the [sorcerers] to their priests so that they would be punished. I believe that if an exemplary punishment was exacted on those sorcerers, God willing, such great evil would end, although as I say, there are now few [sorcerers remaining].

In this land there are different nations and provinces of Indians, each one of which had their own rites, acts, and ceremonies before the Incas subjected them. The Incas abolished some of the rites that they had in those provinces and they instituted new rites.

[Thus,] it is worthwhile knowing the rites described here, so that the idolatries and misfortunates can be extirpated and uprooted from the [Indians]. And thus by the grace of Our Lord, I concluded the inspection that I have in my hands of the parishes and valley of the city of Cuzco, by name.[25]

I end this [account] here, in this indecisive way.[26]

Appendix

EDITIONS OF CRISTÓBAL DE MOLINA'S ACCOUNT OF THE FABLES AND RITES OF THE INCAS (*RELACIÓN DE LAS FÁBULAS Y RITOS DE LOS INCAS*)

The first publication of Molina's work was an English translation by Clements R. Markham in 1873. Markham based his translation on a copy of the Madrid document that had been sent to him by Pascual de Gayangos. The location of Markham's copy is not known. After the publication of Markham's translation, interest in Molina's report grew, and various researchers had additional copies made (Rowe 1953). These copies are now housed in national libraries in Santiago and Lima, as well as in libraries at Yale University and the University of California at Berkeley (Means 1928: 397–398; Rowe 1953: 84; Urbano 2008b: xxix). The first Spanish version of the manuscript was published in 1913 and was based on a copy sent to Chile (Molina 1913). Additional Spanish versions were published in 1916, 1943, and 1947—all three of which are based on a copy of Molina's document housed in Lima. More recently, in 1989 and 2008, two versions of Molina's work have been published using the Madrid document. The later of these provides a paleographic version of the text as well as a standardized version.

1873   "An account of the fables and rites of the Yncas." In *Narratives of the Rites and Laws of the Yncas*. Translated from the original Spanish manuscripts and edited with notes and an introduction by Clements R. Markham. First series, no. 48: 1–64. London: Hakluyt Society. Reprinted 1963, 1964, 1969, and 2001.

1913   "Relación de las fábulas y ritos de los incas." Edited by Tomás Thayer Ojeda. *Revista chilena de historia y geografía* (Santiago) 3(5): 117–190.

1916   *Relación de las fábulas y ritos de los incas . . .* Annotations and concordances by Horacio H. Urteaga, biographical and bibliographical information by Carlos A. Romero. Colección de Libros y Documentos Referentes a la Historia del Perú, first series, 1: 1–103. Lima: Sanmartí.

1943   *Fábulas y ritos de los incas . . .* In *Las crónicas de los Molinas*. Biobibliographical prologue by Carlos A. Romero, bibliographical epilogue by Raúl Porras Barrenechea, annotations and short commentaries by Francisco A. Loayza. Los Pequeños Grandes Libros de Historia Americana 1(4): 5–84. Lima: Librería e Imprenta D. Miranda.

1947   *Ritos y fábulas de los incas.* Prologue by Ernesto Morales. Colección Eurindia, no. 2. Buenos Aires: Editorial Futura.

1989   *Relación de las fábulas i ritos de los ingas.* In *Fábulas y mitos de los incas,* edited by Henrique Urbano and Pierre Duviols. Crónicas de América 48: 47–134. Madrid: Historia 16.

2008   *Relación de las fábulas y ritos de los incas.* Edited, with commentary and notes by Julio Calvo Pérez and Henrique Urbano. Lima: Universidad de San Martín de Porres Press.

NOTES

PREFACE

1. The margin notes found on Molina's document are very similar to some recorded on Joan de Santa Cruz Pachacuti Yamqui Salcamaygua's *Relación de antigüedades deste reyno del Pirú* (ca. 1613), which is contained in the same volume (see Duviols and Itier 1993), and may reflect the same hand.

2. These inconsistencies most certainly reflect the insecurity of the copyist and not the linguistic skills of Molina (Porras Barrenechea 1986).

3. We have also standardized the spelling of *ayllo, cacique, chacra,* Citua, *huaca, inti, mitimas, mullu,* Onqoy, *quipu, raymi, sanco,* and *taqui.*

INTRODUCTION

1. Very few Quechua prayers were recorded in the early Colonial Period. Consequently, the prayers offered by Molina have been the subject of intensive study by various scholars, including Castro (1921); Rojas (1937); Farfán Ayerbe and Benigno (1945); Rowe (1953, 1970); Meneses (1965); Beyersdorff (1992); and Calvo Pérez and Urbano (2008).

2. There is some confusion in the identification of the Cuzqueño priest Cristóbal de Molina in early documents, since there were a number of other individuals with the same name living during the early Colonial Period (Rivera Serna 1949). Several of these individuals lived in the city of Cuzco and were close relatives of Cristóbal de Molina (ca. 1529–1586). Most recently, Urbano (1990) has published a series of archival records from Cuzco that have added to our general understanding of Molina's life and those of his relatives who shared similar names.

3. Molina gives various estimates of his age in different documents (Porras Barrenechea 1986: 350; also see Millones 1990: 180, 224).

4. Molina's skills in Quechua were such that the first modern researchers investigating his life suggested that Molina might have been of European-Andean descent. Subsequent documents have revealed that this was not the case.

5. Rivera Serna (1949: 592) states that Molina finished a second visitation of the Cuzco region on 6 August 1576.

6. Molina was also interviewed briefly concerning the laws of the Incas on 2 April 1582 (Córdoba Mexía 1925: 279–281).

7. Also known as Pachacuti Inca Yupanqui.

8. Lists of sayings may have been a common part of Inca oral history, as Garcilaso de la Vega (1966: 396–397), copying from Blas Valera, also provides a list of sayings from Pachacuti Inca Yupanqui.

9. Various researchers have also suggested that Molina's *History of the Incas* may have been a source used by Martín de Murúa. However, since Murúa used Cabello Valboa, as well as a host of other chroniclers, the exact role that Molina's *History of the Incas* played in Murúa's writing is not clear. For a detailed discussion on Murúa and his sources, see Adorno (2008) and Ossio (2008).

10. During his anti-idolatry work in the Ayacucho region (1569–1571), Albornoz charged more than eight thousand natives of being involved with the Taqui Onqoy movement (Millones 1990: 64).

11. Molina also appears to have shared an informant with Juan de Betanzos (1996). Overlapping details are especially clear in their descriptions of the male initiation rite of the Incas.

12. All copies of Olivera's report are now lost. There was certainly a copy in Lima in 1570 (Millones 1990: 63), and another was used by Olivera and Molina in Cuzco in 1577 (Millones 1990: 175-182).

13. At the time of its discovery, the movement was also called Aira (Millones 1990: 63).

14. See MacCormack (1991) for a detailed overview of Andean religious practices at the time of Spanish contact.

15. This inspection of Parinacocha most likely occurred in 1568 while Albornoz was the inspector general of Arequipa.

16. Olivera was the last person to testify on 12 January 1577. The testimonies continued two days later, on 14 January 1577, with a statement by Molina.

17. Spanish fears of indigenous rebellions increased following a failed native uprising in the Jauja region in 1564 (Hemming 1970).

18. Depending on the specific nature of these movements, they can also be classified as "messianic" or "revitalizatic."

19. Andean people have long seen fat as a life-giving force, and it still forms a basic element in many offerings.

20. Cobo (1979: 100) suggests that Acosta may have used Molina's document as one of his sources. This is not correct, although Acosta did rely heavily on Polo de Ondegardo's 1559 manuscript.

CHAPTER ONE

1. Sebastián de Lartaún was the third bishop of Cuzco. He was installed on 4 July 1573 (Esquivel y Navia 1980: 221, 232; Vasco de Contreras y Valverde 1982: 96). Lartaún died in Lima on 9 October 1583 while attending the Third Lima Provincial Council (1582–1583).

2. Molina indicates that his *Account of the Fables and Rites of the Incas* is the second of two reports that he gave to Bishop Lartaún. No copy of the first report has survived, but it is generally referred to as the *History of the Incas*, because it described the lives of the Inca kings. Since both Miguel Cabello Valboa (1951: 258) and Dean Vasco de Contreras y Valverde (1982: 96) note that they used information from Molina's *History of the Incas* while writing their own chronicles, sections of Molina's lost manuscript may be preserved within the folios of these authors' works.

3. Huayna Capac was the last king to rule a united Inca Empire. After his death (ca. 1526), which may have been caused by a European-introduced disease (Cook 1981), a civil war broke out between his two eldest surviving sons, Atahualpa and Huascar. The civil war ended in 1532 with Atahualpa's execution of Huascar, which was followed by Francisco Pizarro's execution of Atahualpa. The following year, Pizarro had Manco Inca, another son of Huayna Capac, coroneted as Inca when the Spaniards entered Cuzco. Manco Inca broke from the Spaniards in 1536, and after a failed attempt to regain control of Cuzco, he retreated into the Vilcabamba region. Manco Inca was murdered in Vilcabamba by Spaniards to whom he had given sanctuary in 1544, but his sons continued to resist Spanish rule until 1572 when Tupac Amaru, Manco Inca's youngest son, was captured and executed by Viceroy Toledo (Hemming 1970).

CHAPTER TWO

1. While discussing the shrines of Cuzco, Cobo (1990: 82) also notes the existence of this temple. It was located southwest of Cuzco in an area that is still called Puquin. House-construction activities in the late 1980s uncovered a large number of cut stone blocks in this area that may have been part of the temple (Bauer 1998: 129–130).

2. Sarmiento de Gamboa (2007: 58) also mentions the painted history

boards of the Incas, and they are referred to in other interviews (Ruiz de Nava-muel 1940a: 140, 173).

3. Cobo (1990: 13–14) used large sections of Molina's description of Inca origin myths in his account.

4. For similar, although not identical, descriptions of the Creator's activities at Tiahuanaco, see Cieza de León (1976), Betanzos (1996), and Sarmiento de Gamboa (2007), among others.

5. Cobo (1979: 104–105) includes part of this account in his work.

6. This object is more frequently spelled as *suntur paucar*. Sarmiento de Gamboa (2007: 65) describes this royal banner as a cross of feathers that hung from a pole, whereas Cobo (1979: 246 [1653: Bk. 12, Ch. 36]) describes it as "a staff, a little shorter than a pike, all covered and adorned from top to bottom with short feathers of various colors which were placed with such skill that they made an elegant effect, and to finish it off, the tips of three large feathers rose up from the top." Guaman Poma de Ayala (1980) provides various drawings of these instruments throughout his chronicle. Cabello Valboa (1951: 274, 290) also mentioned the *suntur paucar* but does not describe it in detail.

7. Here Molina refers to the belief that two other groups, the Tambos and Maras, also emerged from separate caves at Pacaritambo (Bauer 1991). The most detailed version of the Pacaritambo origin myth is provided by Sarmiento de Gamboa (2007). Cabello Valboa (1951) also offers a thorough telling, some of which may have been extracted from Molina's now-lost *History of the Incas*.

8. "Ticsi Viracocha" is written in the left margin of the document.

9. "Idol Huarivillca" is written in the left margin of the document.

10. Huarivilca was the major shrine of the Jauja region.

11. The town of Pucara is located some thirty kilometers from Lake Titicaca in the Province of Puno. Other writers, including Betanzos (1996: 7–10) and Sarmiento de Gamboa (2007: 51–53), suggest that this fabled burning occurred at the town of Racchi, which is in the Province of Cuzco. Also see Cieza de León's (1976: 27–29) description of Viracocha at Racchi.

12. "The deeds of the 2 sons of Pachayachachic or Pachacamac" is written in the right margin of the document.

13. Following current usage, we have elected to translate the word *montañas* as "forested slopes" rather than "mountains." Here Molina is referring to the eastern Andes that drop down toward the Amazonian piedmont.

14. "The origin where some claim to come from" is written in the left margin of the document.

15. Sarmiento de Gamboa (2007: 46–48) includes a similar, although not identical, version of the Cañari origin myth in his chronicle. Numerous Ca-

ñaris were living in the Cuzco region at the time of the Spanish Conquest as a result of Inca colonization policies. Molina and Sarmiento de Gamboa most likely relied on some of these individuals for their descriptions of the Cañari origin myth.

16. This version of the Cañari origin myth was used by Cobo (1990: 14–15).

17. "Origin of the Cañares" is written in the left margin of the document.

18. After having copied Molina's version of this myth into his own work, Cobo provides the following comments:

> Not many years ago, in this city of Lima, I saw a small copper pillar with two *guacamayas* also made of copper perched on top. This piece had been brought from the province of Cañaribamba mentioned above where the Cañaris Indians, in keeping with their paganism, worshiped these copper birds as gods in memory of the fable that has just been told. (Cobo 1990: 15 [1653: Bk. 13, Ch. 2])

19. The site of Ancasmarca is located north of Calca in a side valley of the Vilcanota River Valley (Covey 2006: 178–179).

20. "The origin of other *marcas* [towns]" is written in the right margin of the document.

21. "A month [before] the Flood arrived" is written at the top of the page.

22. That is to say, male llamas or alpacas.

23. Cobo (1990: 16) uses Molina's version of the Ancasmarca origin myth in his chronicle.

24. For additional information on Inca star astronomy, see Zuidema and Urton (1976), Urton (1981), and Bauer and Dearborn (1995).

CHAPTER THREE

1. Here Molina compares *quipus* with rosaries. Cobo (1979: 253) also makes this comparison.

2. Here Molina refers to his *History of the Incas*.

3. This description of Inca Yupanqui and his reverence for the Creator god was used by Cobo (1979: 134–135).

4. Quishuarcancha, the temple of the Creator god in Cuzco, is also mentioned by Albornoz (1984: 204) and Cobo (1990: 58).

5. Garcilaso de la Vega (1966: 197, 749) places the houses of Ortiz de Guzmán and López de Segovia in the same general area of Cuzco, between the central plaza and the Coricancha.

6. This description of the Creator god and Inca Yupanqui's vision at Susurpuquio was used by Cobo (1979: 133–134). The vision is also described in detail by Sarmiento de Gamboa (2007: 108).

7. This Inca settlement is generally known as Caquia Xaquixaguana. It is located in the Vilcanota River Valley across the river from the towns of Calca and Lamay.

8. This vision is also described in detail by Sarmiento de Gamboa (2007: 108).

9. That is, a puma.

10. Here Molina refers to his *History of the Incas*.

11. The Temple of Thunder was built in Cuzco near that of the Creator (Bauer 2004: 113, 134).

12. Apparently Molina discussed the laws and customs decreed by Inca Yupanqui in his *History of the Incas*.

13. Huanacauri is the most important mountain in the Cuzco Valley. Its summit held a major shrine for the Incas. It was believed that one of the brothers of Manco Capac, the first mythical Inca, was turned into stone at the summit of Huanacauri. After this transformation, Manco Capac and his surviving siblings entered the Cuzco Valley (Bauer 1996). Molina would have described this shrine early on in his *History of the Incas* while discussing the life of Manco Capac and his mythical journey from Tambotoco to Cuzco.

CHAPTER FOUR

1. "Names and offices of the ministers of idolatry of Cuzco" is written in the right margin of the document.

2. Cobo (1990: 163–165) includes much of Molina's information on sorcerers in his own work. Also see Polo de Ondegardo (1916) for many additional details.

3. In a ritual act called *calpa*, the Incas inflated and read the lungs of sacrificed animals as a form of divination. See Polo de Ondegardo (1916), Cabello Valboa (1951), and Sarmiento de Gamboa (2007) for additional descriptions of this ritual.

4. "Virapiricuc" is written in the margin of the document.

5. The words *tell* and *hired* have been crossed out in the document and replaced with the words *see* and *asked*, respectively.

6. Also see Cabello Valboa (1951: 289).

7. "Achicoc—fortune-tellers" is written in the margin of the document.

8. "Camasca" is written in the margin of the document.

9. The town of Huaro is located approximately forty-five kilometers southeast of Cuzco. Cobo (1990: 170) also notes that the inhabitants of Huaro were skilled sorcerers.

10. "Yacarcaes of Huaro" is written in the right margin of the document.

11. Cobo (1990: 169–170) provides similar, although in some parts not identical, information on the workings of the *yacarcaes*.

12. "Other masters of idolatry" is written in the right margin of the document.

13. Parts of this paragraph were used by Cobo (1990: 123–124). For additional information on the so-called confessions of the Incas, see Polo de Ondegardo (1916: 12–14).

14. Cobo (1990: 122) includes this information about sins in his work.

CHAPTER FIVE

1. All of Molina's ritual descriptions are off by one month. For example, those rituals that are generally thought to have occurred in June are listed by Molina under May, and those celebrations that are thought to have occurred in December are listed in November.

2. Molina describes the year as beginning with a new moon within a few days of mid-May. Because his months are off by one month, we should read this as the year beginning around mid-June. This seems to be a general reference to the time of the 21 June solstice (near 25 June in the Gregorian calendar).

3. The Inti Raymi celebration took place around the time of the June solstice.

4. The word *paco* is generally used to refer to male alpacas.

5. Molina provides various versions of this idol's name.

6. Ramos Gavilán (1967: 146) also notes that *canipos* were metal disks.

7. "Prayer to the sun and other idols" is written in the right margin of the document.

8. Cobo (1990: 120) includes a copy of this prayer in his work.

9. Here Molina refers to his now-lost work and notes that it contained a description of the shrine of Huanacauri.

10. Cobo (1990: 158) notes that only members from the Tarpuntay *ayllo* could be priests of the Sun, so they were called by this name.

11. The modern location of this shrine is not known.

12. "Confessions they tell" is written in the right margin of the document.

13. "Paucarruncu" is written in the left margin of the document.

14. Zuidema (1982) was the first to trace this long-distance pilgrimage from Cuzco to the Vilcanota pass.

15. This is most likely the mountain now called Moto (Bauer and Dearborn 1995: 15, 91, 92; Bauer 1999: 108).

16. Modern location unknown.

17. Modern location unknown.

18. Modern Rondocan.

19. Modern Quihuares.

20. Modern Collopata.

21. Modern Pomacanchi.

22. Modern Yanayana.

23. The pass of La Raya divides the Cuzco and the Titicaca drainage systems and marks the source of the Vilcanota River.

24. Modern Lurucache.

25. Modern Sutuc near Sicuani.

26. Modern Racchi.

27. There was a temple built to the Creator god, Viracocha, near the modern town of Racchi.

28. Modern location unknown.

29. Modern Juturoma.

30. Modern Quiquijana.

31. Modern Mollebamba.

32. The hill of Viracochan is located near Urcos. There was a temple at its summit dedicated to the Creator god.

33. There is a small chapel outside the town of Andahuaylillas that is still called Antahuayla.

34. Modern location unknown.

35. Modern location unknown.

36. This may be the hill above the modern town of Quispicanchi called Crus Moqo, which contains petroglyphs as well as evidence of Inca offerings on its surface (Bauer 2004: 36).

37. Molina spells this name as Subcanga. This appears to be the same shrine as Succanca, where the ritual began.

38. Mantucalla was an important temple area outside of Cuzco (Bauer 1999: 81–82).

39. The words "Palpasillo" and "Inca Oillo" are underlined in the document. These two female statues are also mentioned by Molina in his description of the Citua ritual.

40. Acosta (2002: 290) also mentions the use of red blankets on sacrificial llamas.

41. This refers to the cave of Tambotoco at Pacaritambo, the mythical origin place of the Incas. The first Incas are said to have emerged from this cave with corn, llamas, and other elements of Inca culture. According to Molina, a fuller description of the Pacaritambo origin myth was included in his *History of the Incas*.

42. "Corinapa—Collquenapa" is written in the right margin of the manuscript.

43. Parts of this paragraph were copied by Cobo (1990: 142–143) and included in his description of the month of Inti Raymi.

44. Haucaypata was the central plaza of Cuzco.

45. Acosta (2002: 316) also mentions the practice of casting bird feathers on the path where the Inca walked.

46. In the central Andes, agricultural fields are irrigated before the crops are planted.

47. Several other early colonial writers also mention fasting. For example, Cieza de León writes:

> And to celebrate this feast with greater devotion and solemnity, it is said that they fasted for ten or twelve days, refraining from eating much and sleeping with their women, and drinking chicha only in the morning, which is when they eat, and then during the day taking only water, and no hot pepper, or keeping anything in their mouth and other proscriptions which they observe in such fasts. (Cieza de León 1976: 182 [1554: Pt. 2, Ch. 30])

Guaman Poma de Ayala writes:

> In times of fasting and pestilence no one is to eat salt, chile peppers, meat, fruit nor drink chicha, nor eat any food except raw, white maize. (2009: 145 [ca. 1615: 190 (192)])

48. Parts of this paragraph are copied by Cobo (1990: 125, 144).

49. There may have been a blank space in the document and the words "and danced" were filled in later.

50. This plaza was also called Rimacpampa. It is a well-known open space in southeast Cuzco.

51. The word *quispe* [crystal] appears to be a transcription error (Calvo Pérez and Urbano 2008: 40); perhaps the word should be *quilla* [month/moon].

52. Cobo (1990: 145–148) includes a long description of the Citua ritual, most of which is extracted from Molina.

53. Both Sarmiento de Gamboa (2007: 119) and Betanzos (1996: 66), in rare displays of cultural sensitivity, suggest that the Citua was similar to the Iberian ritual of San Juan. During the San Juan celebrations, held on the eve of the June solstice, large bonfires were lit, and individuals cleansed themselves by bathing in the sea. Nevertheless, the Citua, like all Inca ritual practices, was suppressed as the Spaniards gained control over the Andes. The celebration was still practiced, albeit in a dramatically diminished form, in Cuzco in the

1540s and 1550s, while Garcilaso de la Vega was a youth, and he offers a detailed and personalized account of it (1966: 413–417). Garcilaso de la Vega was an eyewitness to various parts of the ritual but, as a child, was not able to see all of it. He writes the following:

> I remember having seen part of this celebration in my childhood. . . . I saw the four Indians running with their spears. I saw the common people shaking their clothes and making the other gestures, and saw them eat the bread called çancu. I saw the torches or pancunu, but did not see the nocturnal rite, because it was very late and I had already gone to bed. (Garcilaso de la Vega 1966: 416 [1609: Pt. 1, Bk. 7, Ch. 7])

Garcilaso de la Vega also notes that the ritual had already lost much of its earlier meaning for the citizens of Cuzco during his childhood:

> . . . in my time the rite was no longer observed with the strict reverence and solemnity of the days of the Incas. It was not performed to banish their ills, for they had already lost their belief in this, but as a memory of olden times. (Garcilaso de la Vega 1966: 416 [1609: Pt. 1, Bk. 7, Ch. 7])

54. This small plaza was called Inti Pata (Plaza of the Sun). It exists today just north of the Coricancha.

55. Quishuarcancha is first written as Quixacarcancha and then corrected.

56. Several other authors mention the locations of these temples (e.g., Garcilaso de la Vega 1966: 197, 424, 427; Albornoz 1984: 204; Cobo 1990: 23). For additional information, see Bauer (1998).

57. Polo de Ondegardo (1916: 18) also notes the Inca practice of removing foreigners from Cuzco during major rituals. This information is copied by Acosta (2002: 314).

58. The Inca nobility inserted large plugs in their earlobes. It was considered bad luck if a lobe broke.

59. An *usño* (also *usñu* and *ushnu*) is generally understood to be a ceremonial platform near the center of Inca towns (Hyslop 1990). However, the Cuzco plaza may have held a different form of *usño,* since several early writers refer to a gold-covered pillar or rock. These include Albornoz (1984: 205), who writes, "Usno was a pillar of gold where they drank to the Sun in the plaza," as well as the Anonymous Chronicler (1906: 158), who notes that a stone pillar and a platform called *usño* stood in the main plaza of Cuzco. Betanzos (1996: 52 [1557: Pt. 1, Ch. 11]) also states that the Cuzco *usño* was a pointed rock covered with gold. Also see Cieza de León (1976: 205–206).

60. The offering of *chicha* was a common element of Inca rituals. Various other authors also describe a well and drainage for liquid offerings in the Cuzco plaza, including Pizarro (1921: 251–252), Garcilaso de la Vega (1966: 358–359), and Cobo (1990: 40, 116). The remains of a similar well and drainage system have been found in a plaza on the Island of the Sun (Stanish and Bauer 2004).

61. The empire of the Incas was divided into four different *suyos*, or geopolitical units, called Antisuyo, Collasuyo, Cuntisuyo, and Chinchaysuyo. Also see MacCormack (1991) and Covey (2006) for discussions of this ritual.

62. Garcilaso de la Vega also saw relays of warriors running from Cuzco during the Citua rituals of this youth:

> The messengers ran with their spears a quarter of a league out of the city, where . . . other Incas, not of the royal blood, but Incas by privilege, took the spears and ran another quarter of a league, and then handed them to others, and so on until they were five or six leagues from the city. . . .
> (Garcilaso de la Vega 1966: 415 [1609: Pt. 1, Bk. 7, Ch. 7])

63. This is at the eastern end of the Cuzco Basin, and is now called "La Angostura" (i.e., The Narrow).

64. Perhaps the modern town of Huacarpay.

65. The shrine of Antahuaylla is also mentioned by Molina in his discussion of May. It was located near the modern town of Andahuaylillas.

66. Located somewhere between modern Andahuaylillas and Quiquijana.

67. Thus the warriors bathed in the Vilcanota River near the modern town of Quiquijana.

68. These kin groups (*ayllos*) are more commonly known as Usca Mayta, Apu Mayta, Hahuanina, Sutic, Maras, and Cuycusa. For information concerning the royal and nonroyal lineages of Cuzco, see Zuidema (1964) and Bauer (1998).

69. These kin groups are more commonly known as Capac, Hatun, Vicaquirao, Chavin Cuzco, Arayraca, and Uro.

70. Location unknown; elsewhere Molina writes "Salpina."

71. Xaquixahuana was located near Anta, west of Cuzco.

72. The mountain of Tilca is located near the town of Marcahuasi in the Limatambo area; see Heffernan (1996).

73. Modern Marcahuasi.

74. That is, "clothes."

75. These warriors bathed in the Apurimac River below the modern town of Limatambo.

76. These kin groups are more commonly known as Sucsu, Aucaylla, Taruntay, and Sañoc.

77. Modern Chitapampa.

78. Modern Pisac.

79. The Cuyo and Paullo (also called Huayllacan) were two ethnic groups that were located north of Cuzco, near Pisac, on either side of the Vilcanota River; see Covey (2006).

80. These warriors bathed in the Vilcanota River beside the modern town of Pisac.

81. These kin groups are more commonly known as Raurau, Chima, Masca, and Quizco.

82. The pass between Cuzco and Yaurisque.

83. The town of Yaurisque is located approximately nine kilometers from Cuzco.

84. The site of Tantar Cuzco is located along the Inca road near the modern town of Paruro.

85. Cusibamba is located beside the Apurimac River in the province of Paruro.

86. During Inca times, the ritualized cleansing of evil ended with the four relays of warriors bathing themselves and their weapons in the major rivers of the region. In the later and more limited rituals witnessed by Garcilaso de la Vega (1966: 415), the Citua event ended with the runners sticking their spears "in the ground as a barrier to prevent the ills from re-entering the area from which they had been banished." The instruments of war, the spears, appear to have been important elements of the ritual, suggesting that the maladies of the city were both carried within the spears and defeated by them.

87. An incomplete word starting with the letters "si" followed by a blank space.

88. Molina notes that during the Citua, people emerged from their houses shaking their blankets and crying out for the illnesses to leave the city and asking for a prosperous year. Garcilaso de la Vega also recalls seeing such events during his youth in Cuzco:

> The inhabitants, men and women, old and young, came to the doors of their houses as the . . . [warriors] ran by and shook their clothes as if shaking out dust, giving vent to loud cries of pleasure and rejoicing. They then ran their hands over their heads and faces, arms, legs, and bodies, as if washing themselves and driving all ills out of their house so that the messengers of the Sun might expel them from the city. This was done not only in the streets through which the [warriors] passed but also throughout the city as a whole. (Garcilaso de la Vega 1966: 415 [1609: Pt. 1, Bk. 7, Ch. 7])

89. The Citua torches intrigued the Spaniards, and we have several different descriptions of them. Polo de Ondegardo states that they were called *panconcos* and that, among other things, the natives hit each other with them. He writes:

> ... the festival called Citua was celebrated in the following manner. They all gathered before the moon came up on the first day, and when they saw it they emitted great shouts, with torches in their hands, crying "Evil be driven out," and hitting one another with the torches. These were called *panconcos*. When this was done, there were general ablutions in the streams and wells, each person in his *seque*, or neighborhood, and they drank for four successive days. (Polo de Ondegardo 1965: 31 [1559/1585])

The Anonymous Chronicler (1906: 158–159 [ca. 1570]) writes of the evening ritual and the use of torches:

> At the conjunction of the moon in that month, for three nights, all the Indians left the plaza together with many wooden torches with grass burning to give light, and they ran through all the streets with great shouts and cries in loud voices, saying that it was to cast the pestilence and sicknesses from the city ... (Our translation)

Guaman Poma de Ayala (2009: 192–193 [1615: 253 (255)]; also see 2009: 221 [1615: 285 (287)]) also provides a good description of the Citua:

> During this month the Inca ordered sickness and pestilence to be banished from the towns of the whole kingdom. Warriors armed as if going to war wave torches shouting, "Sickness and pestilence be gone from among our people and this town! Leave us!" At this time they wash all the houses and streets with water and clean them. They did this throughout the whole kingdom.

The best description, however, is provided by Garcilaso de la Vega:

> The following night they went out with great torches of straw woven like the jackets for oil jars in round balls. These were called pancuncu, and took a long time to burn. Each was fastened to a cord a fathom in length, and they used to run through all the streets trailing the torches till they were outside the city, as if the torches removed the evils by night as the spears did by day. The burned torches were finally cast into the streams that pass through the city, together with the water in which the people

had washed the previous day, so that the running water might carry the ills they had driven out of their houses and out of the city down to the sea. If later any Indian, young or old, found any of these torches in a stream, he would flee from it as if from the flames, lest the evils that had been driven out should attach themselves to him. (Garcilaso de la Vega 1966: 415 [1609: Pt. 1, Bk. 7, Ch. 7])

90. The use of *sanco* during the Citua celebrations is also described by various other authors. Again, Garcilaso de la Vega provides an exceptionally good example:

Shortly before dawn on the night of the baking, all those who had fasted washed their bodies and took a little of the dough mixed with blood and rubbed it on their heads, faces, chests and shoulders, arms and legs, as if cleansing themselves so as to rid their bodies of infirmities. This done, the eldest relative, the master of the house, anointed the lintel of the street door with dough, leaving some sticking to it as a sign that ablution had taken place in the house and that their bodies had been cleansed. (Garcilaso de la Vega 1966: 414 [1609: Pt. 1, Bk. 7, Ch. 6])

91. An incomplete word starting with the letters "ba" followed by a blank space.

92. As in many societies, the Incas mummified their dead rulers and continued to worship them after their death. For additional information on the mummies of the Incas, see MacCormack (1991) and Bauer and Coello Rodríguez (2007).

93. The manuscript contains the word *lana* [wool] instead of the word *huaca*.

94. For an overview of festive activities that took place in Inca plaza, see Morris and Covey (2003).

95. These two female statues are also mentioned in Molina's description of Inti Raymi.

96. Here Molina writes *mochauan*. He uses the Quechua word *muchay* [to adore, to venerate] with the Spanish third-person plural imperfect indicative form *-aban*.

97. Cuzco, like many Andean communities, was divided into moieties, in this case called Upper Cuzco (Hanan Cuzco) and Lower Cuzco (Hurin Cuzco). Each moiety was further divided into an equal number of lineages, generally called *ayllos*.

98. Betanzos (1996: 62) calls these headdresses "*pillaca-llauto.*"

99. This feature of the plaza is also mentioned in Molina's description of the Citua ritual.

100. Cobo (1990: 116) also describes this pouring of *chicha*.

101. Polo de Ondegardo (1916: 23) also mentions that white and wooly camelids were offered during this month.

102. Polo de Ondegardo also describes the use of the blood paste during Inca rituals.

During this month, the *mamaconas* of the Sun made large quantities of cakes with the blood of certain sacrifices. They gave a piece to each of the foreigners and also sent some to the foreign *huacas* throughout the kingdom, and to various Curacas as a sign of alliance and loyalty to the Sun and the Inca. (Polo de Ondegardo 1965: 23 [1559/1585])

103. Those of Hanan Cuzco and Hurin Cuzco.

104. First written as "*alcanba*" and then corrected to "*alcançaua.*"

105. We have followed Calvo Pérez and Urbano's (2008) paleographic edition for the spelling of the words in Molina's Quechua prayers.

106. See Rowe (1953) for alternative translations of Molina's Quechua prayers.

107. This may have been a well-known prayer, since Guaman Poma de Ayala (1980; 2009: 40), Murúa (1987, 2006), Oré (1992), and Santa Cruz Pachacuti Yamqui Salcamaygua (1993) all provide very similar versions (Beyersdorff 1992: 134–137). Cobo (1990: 120) includes a copy of this prayer in his work.

108. The translation of this prayer is complicated by the fact that Molina has inserted explanatory information within it. We have marked the explanatory information by including it within parentheses.

109. The bridge of Chuquichaca spanned the Urubamba River near the modern town of Chaullay. This bridge marked the most important entrance to the Vilcabamba region.

110. Several other writers describe this shrine, including Betanzos (1996: 7–10) and Sarmiento (2007: 52). The shrine to Viracocha was built on top of the mountain now called Viracochan, between the towns of Huaro and Urcos.

111. The area of Amaybamba is located between Ollantaytambo and Chuquichaca.

112. The exact location of Huaypon is not known; however, it may have been located near Lake Huaypo between Maras and Anta.

113. Cobo (1990: 120) includes a copy of this prayer in his work.

114. Molina includes another version of this prayer in his description of the *capacocha*.

115. In this context, the name Tambo refers to the people of the Pacaritambo region, where the first mythical Incas were believed to have emerged.

116. Cobo (1990: 120) includes a similar, although not identical, prayer in his work.

117. Rowe (1956) proposes that the copyist, or perhaps Molina, erroneously skipped from one line of the text to another, leaving out part of this prayer. A more recent study by Calvo Pérez and Urbano (2008: 76–77) suggests that this is not the case.

118. Molina did not translate this phrase.

119. Cobo (1990: 120) includes a similar, although not identical, prayer in his work.

120. This should read "the third day," or the copyist skipped a line.

121. Cieza de León provides a similar account when describing the Capacocha:

> Thus they say that it was the custom of the Incas of Cuzco to have all the statues and figures of the idols in the *huacas*, which were the temples where they worshipped, brought into that city each year. They were transported with great veneration by the priests and *camajocs*, which is the name of the guardians. When they entered the city, they were received with great feasts and processions and lodged in places set aside and appointed for that purpose. And the people having assembled from all parts of the city and even from most of the provinces, men and women, the reigning monarch, accompanied by all the Incas and *orejones*, courtiers and important men of the city, provided great festivals and *taquis*. (Cieza de León 1976: 190–191 [1554: Pt. 2, Ch. 29])

122. This is the second time that Molina records this prayer, although with subtle differences.

123. We have elected to translate the word *pascua*, the Holy Week that ends with Easter, as "holy period."

124. Polo de Ondegardo indicates that parts of the Citua continued long after the conquest:

> The ablutions and drinking bouts and some vestiges of this festival called Citua still survive in some places with slightly changed ceremonies and with great secrecy, although the principal and public part of the celebration is no longer performed. (Polo de Ondegardo 1965: 31 [1559/1585])

125. The town of Oma was located at the eastern end of the Cuzco Valley, near where San Jerónimo is now.

126. Throughout the document, we have elected to translate Molina's term *"caballeros"* (or "knights") as "warriors."

127. During pre-Inca times, the Ayarmaca were concentrated in the Maras region, northwest of Cuzco. They were resettled in various towns across the Cuzco region by the Incas (Rostworowski de Diez Canseco 1970; Covey 2006; Cahill 2007).

128. Betanzos (1996: 68) calls the month of November Cantarai.

129. As elsewhere, here Molina notes that his now-lost work contained a description of the life of Manco Capac.

130. Cobo (1990: 149) uses parts of this paragraph in his description of the month of Ayarmaca.

131. Cobo (1990: 126–134) incorporates most of Molina's discussion of November in his account of the Capac Raymi ritual. For another detailed description of Capac Raymi and the male initiation rite, see Cieza de León (1976: 35–37).

132. The male initiation rite continued to be held after the Spaniards took control of Cuzco. Betanzos, who provides his own detailed description of this ritual, writes:

> . . . they continued doing it that way up to this present year we are in, which is 1551. Though attempts have been made to suppress them in this city of Cuzco, the people go out and secretly perform this fiesta and the others that this lord [Inca Yupanqui] established in the small towns surrounding this city of Cuzco. (Betanzos 1996: 64 [1557: Pt. 1, Ch. 61])

The continuation of the Capac Raymi rituals is also noted by Polo de Ondegardo, who writes:

> During these celebrations the Inca youths were dedicated and were given the *huaras*, or breechcloths, their ears were pierced, they were whipped with nettles by the elders, and their faces were completely smeared with blood as a sign that they were to be loyal knights of the Inca. No stranger was permitted in Cuzco during this month and celebration, and at the end of the festivities all those from the outside came in and were given certain cakes of maize with blood of sacrifices, which they eat as a sign of alliance with the Inca. Various ceremonies were carried out, which, since it is believed that they are no longer performed, will not be described. It will merely be noted that the donning of the *huaras*, or breechcloths, by the youths, who are 12 to 15 years old, is still done today and is widespread among the Indians. (Polo de Ondegardo 1965: 24 [1559/1585])

133. Molina mentions these sandals various times during his description of the Capac Raymi celebration. Betanzos provides additional information on them, telling the reader why this footwear held such an important role in the initiation ritual of young men:

> ... they dress him in that tunic of black wool that those women made him and put on him the shoes made of straw, which the young man will have made while fasting so that they would know that if the young man were in a war and needed shoes he would know how to make them of straw and pursue the enemy with those shoes on. (Betanzos 1996: 61 [1557: Pt. 1, Ch. 61])

134. Betanzos also describes these scarves and headbands, writing:

> After he has the shoes on, they will put a black band around his head. On top of this band they will put a white sling. Around his neck they will tie a white cloak that hangs over his back. The cloak will be narrow, two spans wide, and hang from his head to his feet. (Betanzos 1996: 61 [1557: Pt. 1, Ch. 61])

135. The cutting of hair during this ritual is also mentioned by Betanzos (1996: 61) and Cieza de León (1976: 35).

136. Cobo describes in detail such an act of reverence:

> Facing their gods or their temples and *guacas*, they lowered their heads and their bodies in a profound show of humility, and they would stretch their arms out in front of themselves, keeping them parallel to each other from the beginning to the end, and with the hands open and the palms out, a little above the level of their heads. Then they would make a kissing sound with their lips. Next they would bring their hands to their mouths and kiss the inside of their fingertips. (Cobo 1990: 118 [1653: Bk. 13, Ch. 23])

Polo de Ondegardo provides a similar description of an act of reverence:

> The manner of praying to Viracocha, to the Sun, and to the stars was the same: namely to spread one's hands and make a certain sound with the lips (like a kiss), and to request what each one wanted; and to offer a sacrifice. (Polo de Ondegardo 1965: 6 [1559/1585])

Cieza de León (1976: 183 [1554: Pt. 2, Ch. 30]) also describes this ritual, writing: "Bending their backs and puffing out their cheeks, they blew their breath toward him, making the *mocha*, which is like paying obeisance."

137. Cobo (1990: 29) used this description of the Moon idol in his chronicle.

138. According to Inca mythology, several important events occurred at Matahua during the lives of Manco Inca and his son Cinchi Roca (Cabello Balboa 1951: 263, 264, 268; Cobo 1979: 109). It was located near the base of Huanacauri; see Bauer (1998: 110–112).

139. Betanzos provides a more complete description of these "bunches of straw," writing:

> After this, they will give him a handful of straw as big around as a wrist. The tips of the straw should be pointing up just as it grows. To the other end of this straw, there will be hung a small bunch of long wool, which looks almost like a small amount of long, white hemp. (Betanzos 1996: 61 [1557: Pt. 1, Ch. 61])

140. This is a reference to the Pacaritambo origin myth of the Incas.

141. Location unknown.

142. Flogging and whipping continue to be part of many ritual dances in the Cuzco region.

143. The use of seashells as musical and ritual instruments is still common in the Andes.

144. Detailed descriptions of Inca rituals are extremely rare. Ramos Gavilán does, however, provide a description of the Inca male initiation ritual occurring in the town of Copacabana on the shore of Lake Titicaca. There are clear parallels between the Copacabana ceremony and that conducted in Cuzco:

> At some solemn and joyful celebrations, every group, neighborhood, or *ayllo* would bring their boys, up to thirteen or fourteen years old, more or less, and they would gather them in a public place, where the [children] could be seen by everybody. There they were beaten with certain slings made of animal skins on their feet, arms, and hands, until they shed some blood. Afterward, the principal of that group would scold those beaten [boys], giving them good advice, telling them that they were no longer to live as boys, since they had reached the age at which, as men, they had to concern themselves with things related to the service of their community and of the Inca, their Lord. [Then] those that had been beaten were

brought together and shorn. [Later], they were divided into [groups of] threes or twos on a plain, close to the lake. On a certain signal that was given to them, they all would start a race to the top of the hill, where the judges were awaiting to see who were the winners. The hill still retains the name Llallinaco (since the Olympic games were performed there). To motivate and challenge the boys in running, those who arrived first to the top, at the end of the race, were rewarded. They were given certain silver discs that the Indians used in their *llautos* (that are like their hats), and those discs are called *canipos*; or they were given certain *chuspas* (that are hanging bags, like *tahelíes* [Islamic signs of faith] that cross the chest), which they still use to put coca in. These [*chuspas*] that were given as rewards were extremely curious because they were [made] of *cumbi* and only the principal people were allowed to use them. Those who compete in these Olympic Games were nobles, because the Inca always liked to have himself served by people who were [nobles]. Thus, [the Inca] would employ those who had been successful in those games in honorable offices, like being postmen (that we call here *chasques*), or [he] would make them captains, governors, or [he would place them] in other offices that they held in [high] esteem. [He did so] because the Inca considered them brave [and held them] in high respect, since they had proven themselves. As a sign that he had installed them as nobles, and so that they could be known as such, he had their ears pierced, which was the insignia of nobles and braves. But in these Olympic Games, those who were left behind, exhausted because of their own weaknesses, were scolded by their fathers, relatives, and those of their group, [who] shamed them with harsh words and [they] were even beaten again . . . (Ramos Gavilán 1967: 145–147 [1621: Pt. 1, Ch. 23]; our translation)

145. Betanzos also describes this special clothing:

Once he is in the city, they will dress the neophyte in a red tunic with a white stripe across the middle from bottom to the top of the tunic with a certain blue border at the bottom of the tunic. They will put a red band on his head. (Betanzos 1996: 61 [1557: Pt. 1, Ch. 61])

146. Betanzos also mentions the importance that halberds played in this ritual:

When they are there, the relatives of this neophyte, who are almost like godfathers, will carry some long halberds of gold and silver. After making the sacrifice, they tie that straw they carry in their hands to the heads of the halberds, and hang from the heads of the halberds that wool that was hung on the straw. (Betanzos 1996: 61 [1557: Pt. 1, Ch. 61])

147. Several other early colonial writers mention this place (also spelled Yauraba, Auraba, and Rauaraya) in relation to the initiation rites of young men; see Bauer (1998: 124).

148. The important role that young women played in this ritual is confirmed by Betanzos, who writes:

One month after the beginning of this fast, his relatives should bring him a young maiden who has never known a man. While also on a fast, this maiden will make a certain jug of *chicha*, which will be called *caliz*. The maiden will always walk along with the young man during the sacrifices and fasts. She will serve him as long as the fiesta lasts. The relatives of the neophyte accompany him and the maiden carrying the little jug of *chicha* called *caliz*. . . . As the young man arrives this way where the *guaca* is, with the maiden carrying that little *caliz* jug, she will fill two small tumblers of *chicha* and give them to the neophyte. He will drink one of the tumblers and give the other to the idol by pouring the *chicha* out in front of it. (Betanzos 1996: 61 [1557: Pt. 1, Ch. 61])

149. Location unknown.

150. The mountain of Anaguarque is located between Huanacauri and Cuzco. There is a small plain on the mountain summit with a clear view of Cuzco. The plain contains the remains of a poorly preserved structure and fragments of Inca pottery (Bauer 1998: 120).

151. The towns of Choco and Cachona are located at the base of Anaguarque.

152. Elsewhere written by Molina as Rauraua and Yauraba.

153. Details of this race are also recorded by Betanzos:

Then all of the neophytes there will be brought together and they will all be ordered to leave there all running together with the halberds in their hands as if they were chasing their enemies. This run will be from the *guaca* to a hill where this city comes into view. Certain Indians will wait in this place so that they will see how these neophyte warriors arrive running and who arrives first. The winner will be honored by all his people. They will give him a certain thing and tell him that he did it like a good *orejon* warrior. They will give him the nickname Guaman, which means hawk. (Betanzos 1996: 61–62 [1557: Pt. 1, Ch. 61]).

154. For additional descriptions of this race, see Cieza de León (1976: 35) and Santa Cruz Pachacuti Yamqui Salcamaygua (1950: 221).

155. This hill, written as Rauaraya, is also mentioned as part of the *ceque* system by Cobo (1990: 79 [1653: Bk. 13, Ch. 16]), who writes, "The fourth was called Rauaraya. It is a small hill where the Indians finished running on the feast of the Raymi, and here a certain punishment was given to those who had not run well."

156. Sarmiento de Gamboa (2007: 123) also mentions a Guamancancha. Its exact location is not known; Cobo (1990: 56) suggests that it was near Sacsahuaman, whereas Albornoz (1984: 204) places it above the nearby Cuzco suburb of Carmenca.

157. This shrine was also included within the sacred places of the Cuzco *ceque* system (Bauer 1998: 70). Cobo (1990: 61) notes that this shrine (Apu Yauira) was located on the hill of Piccho, which is immediately to the west of Cuzco, and that people went to it during the festival of Capac Raymi. The shrine is also mentioned by Cieza de León (1976: 35) and Albornoz (1984: 204), both of whom indicate that youths participating in the initiation rites gathered at it several days after their ascents of Huanacauri and Anaguarque. Betanzos provides the following description of the ritual activities that took place at the *huaca* during the male initiation rites:

> The next day they will leave the city for a place where I will point out another *guaca* tomorrow. It will be called Yavira and will be the idol of the favors. When they are there they will have a big fire built and offer to the *guaca* and to the Sun sheep and lambs, beheading them first. With the blood of these animals they will draw a line with much reverence across their faces, from ear to ear. They will also sacrifice in this fire much maize and coca. All of this will be done with great reverence and obeisance in making the offering to the Sun. (Betanzos 1996: 62 [1557: Pt. 1, Ch. 14])

158. Betanzos also describes this special clothing:

> Next right there they will put a very colorful tunic on the neophyte and a very colorful cloak on top of everything. These will be very fine garments. They will put on his ears some large gold earplugs, fastened with red thread. They will place a large gold scallop shell on his chest and put straw shoes on him. They will put a very colorful band around his head, which they call *pillaca-llauto*, and on top of this band they will put a feather diadem and a gold disk. (Betanzos 1987: 62 [1557: Pt. 1, Ch. 14])

159. Betanzos also writes of the beating of the boys during the initial rite:

> This done, they will put a new breechclout on him, which up to that time
> no young man could wear. If by chance he forgot to put it on there, he
> could never wear it again in his life. After this, they will make the neophyte
> hold out his arms, and his relatives, who were waiting there with him like
> godfathers, will beat him on the arms with slings so that he will remember
> and not forget the oath he took there and the favor done him. (Betanzos
> 1987: 62–63 [1557: Pt. 1, Ch. 14])

160. Cabello Balboa (1951: 268) also notes that Sinchi Roca underwent the
male intuition rite. Perhaps this information was taken from Molina's *History
of the Incas*.

161. This description of the puma skin dancers was used by Cobo (1990:
133). For other descriptions of puma skin dancers, see Cieza de León (1976:
36) and Garcilaso de la Vega (1966: 218).

162. Cobo (1990: 133, 142) and Polo de Ondegardo (1916: 21) also mention the *cayo* dance. Polo de Ondegardo's information is later copied by Acosta
(2002: 316) as well as by Ramos Gavilán (1967: 153).

163. Betanzos also describes the puma-skin costumes and the drums used
in this ritual:

> There they will find all the lords of Cuzco dressed in long red tunics that
> come down to their feet. They will have tanned lion skins on their backs,
> the heads of the lions over their own heads and the faces of the lions in
> front of their faces. These lion heads will have gold ear ornaments. These
> lords who are in the square like this will have four gold drums. (Betanzos
> 1996: 63 [1557: Pt. 1, Ch. 61])

164. Calispuquio was an important spring behind the fort of Sacsayhua-
man that is mentioned by various early colonial writers as well as in archival
documents (Bauer 1998: 55). Most importantly, Betanzos also describes the
young male initiates visiting the spring, writing:

> The Inca ordered that after the thirty days had elapsed the relatives of
> these neophytes should assemble there in the square and bring the neo-
> phytes with them. After thrusting the halberd into the ground, the neo-
> phytes remain standing, hold the halberd in their hands, and extend their
> arms; their relatives will then beat them with slings on their arms so that
> they will remember this fiesta. Next they will go from there to a fountain

called Calizpuquio, which means spring of the *caliz*. They will go to this spring, where they all bathe, at nightfall. Then they will put on other fine tunics. (Betanzos 1996: 63 [1557: Pt. 1, Ch. 14])

165. Cobo (1990: 133) includes much of this information in his account of the month of Capac Raymi.

166. Cobo (1990: 117, 134) also mentions the offering of livestock and carved wooden statues. Also see Acosta (2002: 316).

167. Betanzos (1996: 63) also describes the piercing of the boys' ears.

168. This statement echoes the earlier comment of Molina, which indicates that individuals who had broken earlobes were seen as unfortunate and cast from Cuzco during the Citua celebration.

169. Cobo (1990: 132–134) includes an edited version of this information in his account of the month of Capac Raymi.

170. Livestock fertility celebrations are still widely practiced in the Andes.

171. A more literal translation of this sentence reads "They performed this sacrifice for the livestock on the same day across the entire kingdom [blank space] [when] they sprayed with *chicha* for the livestock."

172. Molina also mentions this temple in the beginning of this account.

173. Cobo (1990: 135–138) includes much of this information in his chapter on the month of Camay.

174. These are the cactus fruit commonly called *tunas* (prickly pears, *Opuntia ficus-indica*). Several other writers describe this ritual battle between Hanan and Hurin Cuzco. For example, Betanzos writes:

The next morning all of the neophytes will go out into the square in military formation as if they were going into battle with their slings in their hands. Around their necks they will carry net bags full of *tunas*. The same number will be placed on either side of the square as they start their battle or fight. They will fight this battle with the objective of learning how they should fight their enemies. (Betanzos 1996: 63–64 [1557: Pt. 1, Ch. 14])

175. The ritual use of white feathers from this bird is mentioned by several other early colonial writers; see MacCormack (1990: 137).

176. Betanzos (1996: 60–61 [1557: Pt. 1, Ch. 14]) confirms this period of fasting by the youths, writing: "And he will not eat anything other than raw maize nor will he eat meat, salt, agi peppers, nor have anything to do with a woman."

177. Cobo (1979: 20) includes this quote in his chronicle.

178. Parts of this paragraph were copied by Cobo (1990: 20–21).

179. Because the months started on new moons, the fifteenth evening of each month would have had a full moon.

180. Sarmiento de Gamboa also mentioned this rope, writing:

> They say that, above all, Pachacuti made a thick wool rope of many colors and plaited with gold, with two red tassels at each end. They say it was 150 fathoms long, more or less. It was used in their public festivities, of which there were four principal ones a year . . . In these festivities, they would take the rope from the House or storehouse of the Sun, and all the principal Indians, splendidly dressed, would take hold of it in [hierarchical] order. Thus they would come singing from the House of the Sun to the plaza, and they would completely encircle it with the rope, which was called *moroy urco*. (Sarmiento de Gamboa 2007: 119 [1572: Ch. 31])

For additional information on this rope, see Cieza de León (1976) and Garcilaso de la Vega (1966).

181. *Guasca* was another name for the sacred rope. Cobo explains:

> In order to celebrate on the day of his birth, his father Guayna Capac had a golden chain made very thick and so long that the Indians could dance while holding on to it, instead of holding hands; and there was enough room for two hundred persons to dance with it, spread out like a wing. In memory of this marvelous chain or rope (called *huascar* in their language) the prince was given the name of Huascar. (Cobo 1979: 163 [1653: Bk. 12, Ch. 18])

182. Unknown term. This may be a copyist error.

183. The Saphi River (i.e., Capi Mayo) continues to flow through Cuzco, although it has long been covered over to create modern streets.

184. Puma Chupa, the confluence of the two rivers that flow through Cuzco, is a well-known place.

185. That is, the Atlantic Ocean.

186. Cobo (1990: 136–137) provides a similar, but not identical, description of the offerings made at Puma Chupa and their trip to Ollantaytambo.

187. Cobo (1990: 139–140) uses parts of Molina's description in his own discussion of the month of Hatun Cuzqui and the Aymoray celebration.

188. The arch to which Molina refers is that of Arco Punco (also called Arco de la Plata). The arch was destroyed in the mid-1900s.

189. Most major, and many minor, shrines of the Andes had fields assigned to them. The harvests from those fields were dedicated to the individual shrine cults.

190. Cobo (1990: 140) provides a similar, but not identical, description of these events.

CHAPTER SIX

1. There is a transcription error in the text with information missing.

2. Cobo (1990: 201) uses this information in his description of the Inca birth ritual.

3. First hair cuttings are still widely celebrated in the Andes.

4. Some of this information may have been used by Cobo (1990: 201-202).

5. Cobo (1990: 202–203) copies most of Molina's description of the Quicochico in his own work.

6. Cobo (1990: 206–207) copies most of this paragraph and includes it in his own description of Inca marriages.

CHAPTER SEVEN

1. Cobo (1990: 154–156) copies most of Molina's description of the Capacocha. For another detailed description of this important event, see Cieza de León (1976: 190–193). For modern discussions, see Zuidema (1973), MacCormack (1991), and McEwan and Van de Guchte (1992), among many others.

2. Evidence of Capacocha offerings has been recovered at the summits of various mountains (Reinhard 1983, 1985; Ceruti 2004).

3. This same location is mentioned in Molina's description of the Citua celebration, there spelled Satpina.

4. Here Molina uses the Quechua verb *to adore* (*muchoy*) with the Spanish location indicator (*adero*) to write "*mochadero*" or "place of worship."

5. Cobo (1990: 112–113, 155) copies much of this information into his work.

6. Here Molina uses the Quechua word for shrine (*huaca*) with the Spanish diminutive (*illos*), to write "*huaquillos*," or "little shrines."

7. Cobo (1990: 155–156) incorporates much of this paragraph into his own work.

8. Very few other early colonial writers support the suggestion that the Incas cut the hearts out of their sacrificial victims, and no archaeological evidence has been found to support this statement. The description may have been influenced by accounts of Aztec offerings.

9. The smearing of blood from ear to ear is mentioned by various writers; see Cornejo (2002).

10. Chuquicancha is most likely the ruins that are now called Rumi Huasi Bajo and Rumi Huasi Alto. They are located on a hill above the town of San Sebastián (Bauer 1998: 87–89).

11. Parts of this paragraph were copied by Cobo (1990: 112).

12. Molina provides another transcription of this same prayer earlier in his manuscript.

13. Earlier in his manuscript Molina indicates that this shrine "was shaped like a person, although its face could not be seen."

14. According to Inca origin myths, the very first Incas were four brothers and four sisters who emerged from the cave of Tambotoco at a place called Pacaritambo. One of these mythical brothers was named Ayarcache. This myth is told by many early colonial writers, and it would have been included in the first few chapters of Molina's *History of the Incas*. Cabello Valboa (1951: 256–264) provides an especially long description of the myth as well as Ayarcache's conversion into stone at the top of Huanacauri, which may be based on Molina's earlier account.

15. Here Molina refers to an earlier document concerning the shrines of the Cuzco region that he gave to Bishop Lartaún.

16. Cobo (1990: 156) copies much of this information into his work.

17. Albornoz (1984: 218) also used this term, writing Cachauis.

18. In other words, the priests traveled in straight lines.

19. Cobo (1990: 155–157) copies much of this information into his work.

20. Cobo (1990: 156–157) copies much of this information into his work.

21. This is most likely a transcription error for the word *apachitas*. *Apachitas* are piles of stone made by travelers next to roads on mountain passes.

CHAPTER EIGHT

1. At this point there is an abrupt change in the narration of the document. Molina shifts from describing the rites and rituals of the Incas to discussing a religiously inspired cult, now referred to as the Taqui Onqoy movement, which had recently arisen in the Andes. His major source of information on this subject was a document written by Luis de Olivera, perhaps in 1565, which Molina summarized for Bishop Lartaún.

2. The text contains the word *yronía* (irony). Following Mumford (1998: 151), we have elected to translate it as *disaffection* (*ironía*).

3. Many works have been written concerning this indigenous movement (for example, see Millones 1964, 1990; Ossio 1973; Wachtel 1977; Stern 1982a, 1982b; MacCormack 1991; Mumford 1998).

4. Here Molina refers to Manco Inca and his sons, who had retreated from

Cuzco to the Vilcabamba region in 1537 and who led a forty-year war of resistance against Spanish rule in the Andes.

5. It appears that after mentioning Vilcabamba, Molina became sidetracked from summarizing Olivera's report and mentions an unusual belief that he had seen among the natives and that he also believed originated with the Incas in Vilcabamba.

6. In this passage, Molina documents that the indigenous people of the Andes believed that an ointment, most likely fat, was being extracted by the Spaniards to cure a European disease. This may have been an indigenous reaction to the numerous European diseases that were afflicting the Andean populations in disproportional numbers and severity.

7. There is no support for the claim that the Incas in Vilcabamba were behind any such movement. For much of their time in Vilcabamba, the Incas were in contact with the Spaniards in Cuzco and were involved in extensive negotiations for the end of hostilities.

8. The final Spanish raid into Vilcabamba took place under Viceroy Toledo's orders in 1572. The raid resulted in the capture of Tupac Amaru.

9. Here Molina returns to his summary of Olivera's report on the Taqui Onqoy.

10. The shrine of Pachacamac was located on the coast of Peru just south of modern-day Lima, and the shrine of Titicaca was located on the Island of the Sun in Lake Titicaca (Bauer and Stanish 2001). These were two of the most important shrines in the pre-Hispanic Andes.

11. In this case, the Marquis was Francisco Pizarro.

12. Molina uses the word "*enbixauan*," the root of which comes from the plant "Bija" (*Bixa orellana*) from which a red paint (*achiote*) is made. Also see Barcena (1988).

13. Lusate is an unknown term. Calvo Pérez and Urbano (2008: 130–131) suggest that it could be Portugal (i.e., Lusitania).

14. We have elected to translate *repartimientos* as "provinces."

15. The date [15]75 is a copyist error; the date should be [15]65.

16. Lope García de Castro was the interim governor of Peru from 1564 to 1569. He was responsible for sending Albornoz to Arequipa in 1568 and to Huamanga in 1569–1571 to rid these territories of the Taqui Onqoy.

17. Modern Ayacucho.

18. Only a few months after Lope García de Castro arrived in Lima as the new president of the Audiencia (September 1564), plots for an armed revolt were discovered in Jauja and elsewhere in the highlands; see Hemming (1970).

19. Tupac Amaru, the last of the independent Inca kings, was captured in

the remote area of Vilcabamba in mid-1572. He was executed in Cuzco on orders of Viceroy Toledo on 24 September 1572. Molina, along with several other priests, ministered to Tupac Amaru on the day of his death.

20. Here Molina returns to the central thesis of his manuscript, describing the rites and rituals of the Incas.

21. This should read "purple maize."

22. Cobo (1990: 166) includes much of this information in his account of sorcerers.

23. This cleansing ritual was also performed during the Citua.

24. See Polo de Ondegardo (1916: 12–13) for another description of the so-called confessions among the Incas.

25. At this point, the manuscript ends abruptly.

26. This appears to be a closing note added by the copyist.

GLOSSARY

This glossary of selected Quechua (Q), Aymara (A), and Taino (T) words from Molina's *Account of the Fables and Rites of the Incas* is to aid readers in understanding the various terms used and the bewildering range of spellings found in the document.* Readers who are interested in a comprehensive examination of Molina's Quechua should see Calvo Pérez (2008).

achicoc (Q): A type of diviner.

acso [also *axo*] (Q): Skirt.

alaui: See *araui*.

Amaybamba (Q): A subtropical area approximately seventy-five kilometers northwest of Cuzco.

Anaguarque (Q): An important mountain in the Cuzco Valley.

anan: See *hanan*.

ancallo [also *angallo*] (Q): High-quality clothing for females.

Ancasmarca (Q): An archaeological site located north of Cuzco near Calca.

anco: See *uncu*.

angallo: See *ancallo*.

angas (Q): Blue.

Antisuyo (Q): The northeast quadrant of the Inca Empire.

apachita (Q): Sacred cairn.

Apu [also Apo] (Q): Lord.

Apu Punchao [also Apin Punchao] (Q): Lord Sunlight.

apuscay: See *ayuscay*.

araui [also *alaui*] (Q): A song or poem about an important past event.

Atahualpa (Q): Son of Huayna Capac; the Inca ruler captured and killed by Francisco Pizarro in 1532.

atun: See *hatun*.

Aucaypata: See Haucaypata.

Auraba: See Rauaraya.

axo: See *acso*.

Ayarcache (Q): One of the original Incas, brother of Manco Capac, thought to have emerged from the cave of Tambotoco.

Ayarmaca (Q): An ethnic group located northwest of Cuzco in the area of modern Maras.

ayascay: See *ayuscay*.

ayllo (Q): Kin group.

aymoray (Q): To harvest.

ayuscay [also *apuscay, ayascay*] (Q): Birth celebration.

Cachaguaes [also Cacha Guaco] (?): Another name for the Capacocha ritual.

Cachona (Q): A village located south of Cuzco near the base of Anaguarque.

caçico (?): Unknown term.

Caciona: See Cachona.

cacique (T): Local lord.

calejapa: See *caliz*.

caliz [also *calej, calli, calix*] (Q): Health.

Caliz Puquio (Q): Spring of good health.

calpa (Q): Divination by reading the internal organs of sacrificed animals.

calpariçu (Q): An individual who reads the internal organs of sacrificed animals for signs of the future.

camantera (Q): An Andean bird.

camasca (Q): A type of shaman.

camayo [also *camajoc*] (Q): Attendant; specialist.

Cañaris [also Cañares]: An ethnic group of Ecuador.

cancha (Q): An enclosure that may contain several rooms or buildings.

çanco: See *sanco*.

canipo (Q): Metal plate or disk.

cantaray (Q): A method of making *chicha*.

capac (Q): Royal.

Capac Raymi (Q): Royal Celebration; the ritual month including the December solstice.

Capacocha [also Cepacocha] (Q): Royal Offering; a ritual held at a time of great need or to mark a special event such as the coronation of a king.

capi: See *saphi*.

Caquia Xaquixaguana (Q): An Inca town located near Calca and Lamay in the Vilcanota River Valley. It is now called Huchuy Cuzco.

cara [also *çara*]: See *sara*.

caycho (?): Unknown term.

cayo [also *coyo*] (Q): A type of dance.

Cepacocha: See Capacocha.

ceque (Q): Line, division.

chacma (Q): Plow.

chacra (Q): Agricultural field.

chaguar (Q): Maguey.

champi (Q): Metal; axe head.

chapayguanlo: See *chupay huayllo*.

chicha (T?): An alcoholic drink made from maize.

Chinchaysuyo (Q): The northwest quadrant of the Inca Empire.

chipana (Q): Foil; thin metal; bracelet.

choca naco (Q): See *chuqanakuy*.

Choco (Q): A village located south of Cuzco near the base of Anaguarque.

chumpi (Q): Chestnut brown; extremely fine wool, generally from *huanacos*.

chumpi cacico [perhaps *chumpi uncu*] (Q): Chestnut brown tunic?

chupa (Q): Tail.

chupa yacolla (Q): Tail scarf.

chupasita: See *apachita*.

chupay huayllo [also *chupay guayllo, chapayguanlo*] (Q): Tail song.

chuqanakuy [also *chocanaco*] (Q): To be stoned.

chuquecunya [perhaps *chuquicunca*] (Q?): Gold neck?

chuqui (Q): Gold.

Chuqui Ylla Yllapa [also Chuqueylla, Chuquiylla, Chuquillo Yllapa, Chuqui Illapa, Chuquilla, Chuqui Illa, and Chuqui Ylla] (Q): The Inca god of thunder and lightning.

Chuquicancha (Q): A sacrifice area near Cuzco.

Chuquichaca (Q): Golden bridge. One of the major bridges leading into the Vilcabamba region.

chuspa (Q): A small shoulder bag.

Cinchi Roca (Q): The second Inca, son of Manco Capac.

Citua [also Çitua, Situa] (Q): A ritual cleansing held each year in Cuzco.

cocha (Q): Lake.

cochelli (?): Unknown term.

coco (Q): Cactus fruit commonly known as prickly pear.

coi: See *cuy*.

colcapata [perhaps *collquipata*] (Q): Silver disk?

Collasuyo (Q): The southeast quadrant of the Inca Empire.

collca [also *collca*; perhaps *collqui*] (Q): Silver?

collca uncu [also *collca onco*; perhaps *collqui uncu*] (Q): Tunic with silver bangles?

colle [also *colli*] (Q): Dark purple.

colle chicha (Q): Dark purple *chicha*.

collesara [also *culli cara*] (Q): Dark purple maize.

colquenapa [also *colquinapa, colqui napa*] (Q): Silver sacred llama.

colqui [also *colque*] (Q): Silver.

coñanaco (Q): Unknown term.

concho (Q): Sediment.

cori (Q): Gold.

Coricancha (Q): Golden Enclosure, also called the Temple of the Sun, located in the center of Cuzco.

corinapa [also *cori napa*] (Q): Gold sacred llama.

coya (Q): Principal wife of the Inca; queen; noblewoman.

Coya Pacssa [Coya Pacsi] (A): Queen Moon.

coyo: See *cayo*.

cuma cara (Q): Red and yellow maize.

Cuntisuyo (Q): The southwest quadrant of the Inca Empire.

cupa: See *chupa*.

cupay: See *supay*.

curaca (Q): Local lord.

cuy [also *coi*] (Q): Guinea pig.

cuya: See Qoya.

cuychi lliclla (Q): Rainbow mantle.

cuyllo (Q): Bright white; star.

Cuyo (Q): An ethnic group located north of Cuzco around modern Pisac.

Cuzco (Q): Capital city of the Incas.

cuzco axo (Q): Cuzco skirt.

guacamaya [also *guacamayo*]: See *huacamaya*.

guacapanco: See *huaca punco*.

gualanbabi [perhaps *hualanpaui*] (Q): A large, round feathered adornment.

guallina: See *huaylli*.

guaman (Q): Hawk.

Guamancancha (Q): Hawk enclosure.

guanaco [also *huanaco*] (Q): Wild member of the Camelid family.

guara (Q): Loincloth.

guaraca [also *guaraça*] (Q): Sling.

guarachico [also *guarachillo*] (Q): Male initiation rite of the Incas; it included giving the initiates loincloths and having their ears pierced.

guari [also *guarita*] (Q): A type of dance.

guasca [also *huascar*] (Q): A multicolored rope used in Inca rituals. It was also known as Moro Urco.

guayliaquipa [also *gayllaiquipac*] (Q?): Shell trumpet.

hanan [also *anan*] (Q): Upper.

hatun [also *atun*] (Q): Great.

Haucaypata [also Aucaypata] (Q): The central plaza of Cuzco.

hillacunya [perhaps *vilcacunga*] (Q?): Sacred neck?

hongo: See *onqoy*.

huaca (Q): Shrine; sacred location or object.

huaca punco (Q): Shrine opening.

huacacamayo (Q): Shrine specialist; guardian of a *huaca*.

huacamaya [also *guacamaya*, *guacamayo*] (T): Macaw.

huacarpaña [perhaps *huacar paco*] (Q): White alpaca.

Huamanga (Q): Modern Ayacucho.

Huanacauri (Q): An important mountain shrine in the Cuzco Valley.

huanaco: See *guanaco*.

huara: See *guara*.

huaraca: See *guaraca*.

Huarivilca [also Huariuilca, Huarivillca] (Q): The most important shrine of the Jauja region.

Huaro (Q): A town located approximately forty-five kilometers southeast of Cuzco.

Huascar [also Guasca] (Q): Son of Huayna Capac. He briefly ruled Cuzco between ca. 1526 and 1532. He was involved in a civil war with his half brother, Atahualpa, for control of the Inca Empire when the Spaniards invaded Peru.

huaylli [also *guallina*, *huallina*, *huayllina*]: chant; song; singing dance.

huayna (Q): Young.

Huayna Capac (Q): The last Inca to rule over a united empire. He is thought to have died around 1526 on the eve of the Spanish invasion.

Huayna Punchao (Q): Young sunlight, daylight.

huillca: See *villca*.

Huiracocha: See Viracocha.

hurin (Q): Lower.

ichu [also *ychu*] (Q): Mountain grass.

Inca Ocllo [also Inca Oillo] (Q): Noble Inca woman.

Inca Yupanqui: See Pachacuti Inca Yupanqui.

inti (Q): Sun.

Inti Raymi [also Intip Raymi] (Q): Celebration of the Sun. This ritual month included the June solstice.

Jaquijahuana: See Caquia Xaquixaguana.

Limapampa [also Rimacpampa] (Q): A plaza on the southeastern edge of Cuzco.

llahuayra: See *yaguayra*.

llana: See *yana*.

llanca llama [perhaps *yana llama*] (Q): Black llama; dark llama.

llancapata [perhaps *llacsapata*] (Q): Copper disk.

llauto [also *llayto*] (Q): Headband; headdress.

lliclla (Q): A mantle, frequently used by women to carry items.

llipta (Q): A mixture of ash and other ingredients used as a catalyst while chewing coca.

longo: See *runco*.

maio: See *mayu*.

Maiucati: See Mayucati.

mama (Q): Mother.

Mama Huaco (Q): One of the first mythical Incas, sister-wife to Manco Capac.

Mamacocha (Q): Mother lake, sea.

mamacona (Q): Holy woman; woman of the Sun.

Manco Capac (Q): The first mythical Inca. He is believed to have emerged from the cave of Tambotoco.

Manco Inca (Q): Son of Huayna Capac, appointed as ruler of the Incas by Francisco Pizarro. Manco Inca later fought against the Spaniards and retreated into the mountain area of Vilcabamba.

Mantucalla (Q): An important temple complex on the northwest outskirts of Cuzco.

marca [A]: Town, community, place.

mauro pancunco: See *muru pancuncu*.

mayu [also *mayo, maio, maiu*] (Q): River.

Mayocati [also Maiucati] (Q): To follow the river.

mirca (Q): Something of mixed or many colors.

mirca uncu (Q): Multicolored tunic.

mitima (Q; pl., *mitimas, mitimaes*): Colonist; settler.

mocha: See *mucha*.

Moro Urco [also Moro Vrcu, Moroy Urco] (Q): A multicolored rope that was used in important rituals in Cuzco. Also called Guasca.

mucha [also *mocha*] (Q): Adoration, veneration.

mullu (Q): *Spondylus* shells.

mullu mullu (Q): Many *Spondylus* shells.

muru [also *moro*] (Q): Multicolored, spotted.

muru pancuncu [also *mauro pancunco*] (Q): Balls of straw that were lit on fire and used during major celebrations in Cuzco.

napa (Q): A llama used as an insignia of the royal Incas.

ñusta (Q): Princess.

ñusta callixapa (Q): Health princess.

ojota (Q): Sandal.

Ollantaytambo (Q): An important town approximately forty kilometers northwest of Cuzco.

Oma (Q): A town located in the Cuzco Basin near modern San Jerónimo.

Omac Raymi (Q): Celebration of the town of Oma.

onco: See *uncu*.

ongo: See *runco*.

onqoy [also *hongo*] (Q): Sickness.

ooja: See *qoya*.

oque (Q): Gray.

oquipaco (Q): Gray alpaca.

Pacaritambo (Q): House of Dawn; the origin place of the Incas.

Pachacamac (Q): The largest shrine on the coast of Peru.

Pachacuti Inca Yupanqui: The ninth Inca, traditionally believed to be responsible for the initial expansion of the empire. He was also called Inca Yupanqui.

Pachayachachi (Q): One of various names for the Creator god.

paco (Q): Alpaca.

palla (Q): Noblewoman.

palla ayllo (Q): Noblewoman lineage.

Palla Ocllo [also Palpasillo] (Q): Noblewoman.

panaca (Q): Royal lineage.

pancunco: See *muru pancuncu*.

paracay (Q): White.

paro (Q): Dark yellow.

Passa Mama (A): Mother Moon.

paucar (Q): Multicolored, brightly colored.

paucar onco (Q): Multicolored tunic.

paucarpaco (Q): Multicolored alpaca.

paucarquintu [also *parcarquinto*] (Q): Multicolored cluster.

paucarrunco [also *paucar ongo*] (Q): Multicolored basket.

Paullo (Q): An ethnic group located north of Cuzco near modern Paullo.

pechio: See *pisco*.

pilco [also *pielco, pilo*] (Q): An Andean bird.

pilco casa [also *pilco cassa, piloyaco*] (Q): A diadem made with *pilco* feathers.

pilco ruco [also *pilco longo*] (Q): Bag of *pilco* feathers.

piloyaco: See *pilco casa*.

Pisac (Q): A town northeast of Cuzco in the Vilcanota River Valley.

pisco [also *pechio*] (Q): A small bird.

Pizarro, Francisco: Leader of the Spanish Conquest forces.

poca: See *puca*.

Pomapi Chupa: See Puma Chupa.

Poquen Cancha (Q): A Sun temple located in the area of Cuzco now called Puquin.

puca (Q): A shade of red.

Pucamarca [also Pocamarca] (Q): Red town, a temple of the thunder and lightning god located in Cuzco.

pucay (Q?): Unknown term.

Puma Chupa [also Pomapi Chupa] (Q): Tail of the Puma; the confluence of two rivers that flowed through Cuzco.

puna (Q): High grassland areas of the central Andes generally used for pasturing animals.

Punchao (Q): An image of the sun; sunlight; day.

punco (Q): Door or opening.

puquio (Q): Spring.

qoya [also *ooja, coyu*] (Q): A native grass used for cordage.

quepa (Q): Trumpet.

Quicochico [also Ticochico]: Female initiation rite performed when a woman had her first period.

Quilla [also Quilapi] (Q): Moon.

quinto (Q): A small group, cluster.

quipu [also *quipo*] (Q): A knotted cord used for encoding information.

quipocamayo [also *quipucamaio*] (Q): *Quipu* specialist; record keeper.

quirao (Q): Cradle.

quishuar (Q): An Andean tree.

Quishuarcancha (Q): Temple of the Creator god in Cuzco.

quispe (Q): Crystal.

quito (Q): An Andean bird.

quitotica (Q): Feathers of the *quito* bird; headdress made of same.

Rauaraya [also Auraba, Rauraua, Yauraba] (Q): To burn continually. A hill that marked the end of a race run during the male initiation rite.

Raymi (Q): Celebration, ritual, festival.

raymi napa (Q): Sacred ritual llama.

Rotuchico: See Rutuchico.

runco [also *longo, ongo*] (Q): Basket.

Rutuchico [also *rotuchico*] (Q): A ritual involving the first hair cutting of a child.

sanco [also *çanco*] (Q): A maize paste used during rituals; also see *yahuarcanco*.

saphi [also *capi*] (Q): Root.

sara [also *cara, çara*] (Q): Maize.

Sinchi Roca (Q): The second Inca, son of Manco Capac.

Situa: See Citua.

suntur paucar [also *sumtur paucar, suncur paucar, sunctur paucar*] (Q): Royal banner of the Inca made with colorful feathers.

supa yacolla: See *chupa yacolla*.

supay (Q): Demon.

Susurpuquio (Q): A spring where Inca Yupanqui is believed to have had a vision of the Creator god.

suyo (Q): Region; a division of the Inca Empire.

Tambotoco (Q): The cave from which the first mythical Incas emerged.

taqui (Q): Dance.

taqui huallina (Q): Dance chant.

Taqui Onqoy (Q): Dance Sickness. A short-lived millenarian movement of the central Andes of Peru (ca. 1564–1572). Followers of the movement believed that the shrines of the region would rise up and destroy the Spaniards.

tarpuntaes (Q): A class of priests from the Tarpuntay *ayllo*.

tarpuy (Q): To sow.

Tiahuanaco (A): An ancient city near Lake Titicaca (ca. AD 500–1000). The city was in ruins by the time the Incas expanded into the region.

tica (Q): Plumage.

Ticochico: See Quicochico.

Ticsi Viracocha: See Viracocha.

toca (Q?): Unknown term.

toco (Q): Cave or window.

tocto (Q): An Andean bird.

topa (Q): Splendid.

topa yauri (Q): Splendid scepter.

topaguanaco (Q): Splendid guanaco.

Tupac Amaru (Q): Youngest son of Manco Inca. He was captured in Vilcabamba and executed by Viceroy Toledo in Cuzco in 1572.

uauaclla (Q?): Unknown term. Molina used this term for a specific kind of tunic.

Uiracocha: See Viracocha.

uirapiricoc: See *virapiricoc*.

uncu [also *anco, onco*] (Q): A tunic worn by males.

urco [also *urcu*] (Q): Mountain.

Urcos (Q): A town approximately forty-five kilometers east of Cuzco.

ushnu [also *usño, usñu*] (Q): Ceremonial platform.

vilca [also *uilca*] (Q): Sacred.

Vilcabamba (Q): A mountainous area northwest of Cuzco from which the Incas waged a war against the Spaniards (1537–1572).

vilcacamayo [also *vilcacamaio*] (Q): Shrine keeper, shrine specialist.

vira (Q): Tallow, fat, grease.

Viracocha [also Uiracocha, Viracochan, Uiracocha, Huiracocha, Ticsi Viracocha, Ticci Viracocha, Titiuiracochan] (Q): The Creator god of the Incas. Also called by various other name, including Viracocha Pachayachachi.

Viracocha Inca (Q): The eighth Inca ruler and father of Pachacuti Inca Yupanqui.

virapiricoc (Q): An individual who reads the fat of sacrificed animals for signs of the future.

vmisca: See *mirca*.

yabayra: See *yaguayra*.

yacarca (Q): A type of diviner.

yacolla (Q): A cape or scarf.

yaguarcanco: See *yahuarsanco*.

yaguayra [also *llahuayra, yabayra, yahuayra*] (Q?): A type of dance.

yahuar (Q): Blood.

yahuarsanco [also *yaguarcanco, yahuarcanco*] (Q): A mixture of blood and cornmeal used in offerings and during rituals.

yana (Q): Black.

Yauira [also Yavira] (Q): A shrine on the slope of Picchu mountain, just outside of Cuzco.

Yauraba: See Rauaraya.

yauri (Q): A staff.

Yavira: See Yauira.

ychu: See *ichu*.

yllapa (Q): Lightning.

ymaymana [also *ymaimana*] (Q): All kinds of a thing.

ymaymana mullu (Q): All kinds of *mullu*.

---

* We have not attempted to provide glosses for the words included in Molina's transcriptions of Quechua prayers. Readers interested in these prayers may consult Calvo Pérez and Urbano (2008) and various other studies (Castro 1921; Rojas 1937; Farfán Ayerbe 1945; Rowe 1953, 1970; Beyersdorff 1992).

BIBLIOGRAPHY

Acosta, José de

2002   *Natural and moral history of the Indies* [1590]. Edited by Jane E. Mangan, with an introduction and commentary by Walter D. Mignolo. Translated by Frances López-Morillas. Durham: Duke University Press.

Adorno, Rolena

2008   Censorship and approbation in Murúa's *Historia general del Piru*. In *The Getty Murúa*, edited by Thomas B. F. Cummins and Barbara Anderson, 95–124. Los Angeles: Getty Research Institute.

Albornoz, Cristóbal de

1984   Instrucción para descubrir todas las guacas del Pirú y sus camayos y haziendas [ca. 1582]. In "Albornoz y el espacio ritual andino prehispánico," edited by Pierre Duviols. *Revista andina* 2(1): 169–222.

Anonymous Chronicler

1906   Discurso de la sucesión y gobierno de los yngas [ca. 1570]. In *Juicio de límites entre el Perú y Bolivia; prueba peruana presentada al gobierno de la República Argentina*, vol. 8, edited by Víctor M. Maúrtua, 149–165. Madrid: Tipografía de los Hijos de M. G. Hernández.

Ávila, Francisco de

1966   *Dioses y hombres de Huarochirí; narración quechua recogida por Francisco de Ávila* [1598?]. Translated by José María Arguedas. Lima: Museo Nacional de Historia y el Instituto de Estudios Peruanos.

Bandelier, Adolph F. A.

1910   *The Islands of Titicaca and Koati*. New York: The Hispanic Society of America.

Barcena, Roberto

1988   Pigmentos en el ritual funerario de la momia del Co. Anconcagua (Provincia de Mendoza, República Argentina). *Xama* 2: 61–116.

Bauer, Brian S.

1991   Pacariqtambo and the mythical origins of the Inca. *Latin American Antiquity* 2(1): 7–26.

1992   *The development of the Inca state.* Austin: University of Texas Press.

1996   The legitimization of the Inca state in myth and ritual. *American Anthropologist* 98(2): 327–337.

1998   *The sacred landscape of the Inca: The Cuzco ceque system.* Austin: University of Texas Press.

1999   The original ceque manuscript. *Journal of the Steward Anthropological Society* 25(1 and 2): 277–298.

2004   *Ancient Cuzco: Heartland of the Inca.* Austin: University of Texas Press.

Bauer, Brian S., and Antonio Coello Rodríguez

2007   *The Hospital of San Andrés (Lima, Peru) and the search for the royal mummies of the Incas. Fieldiana Anthropology.* New Series No. 39. Chicago: Field Museum of Natural History.

Bauer, Brian S., and David S. P. Dearborn

1995   *Astronomy and empire in the ancient Andes.* Austin: University of Texas Press.

Bauer, Brian S., and Charles Stanish

2001   *Ritual and pilgrimage in the ancient Andes: The Islands of the Sun and the Moon.* Austin: University of Texas Press.

Betanzos, Juan de

1996   *Narrative of the Incas* [1557]. Translated and edited by Roland Hamilton and Dana Buchanan from the Palma de Mallorca manuscript. Austin: University of Texas Press.

Beyersdorff, Margot

1992   Ritual gesture to poetic text in the Christianization of the Andes. *Journal of Latin American Lore* 18: 125–161.

Cabello Valboa, Miguel

1951   *Miscelánea antártica, una historia del Perú antiguo* [1586]. Edited by L. E. Valcárcel. Lima: Universidad Nacional Mayor de San Marcos, Instituto de Etnología.

Cahill, David

2007   Intersections: Economy, political culture, and gendered lives in the Andes. *Ethnohistory* 54(2): 345–353.

Calancha, Antonio de la

1981   *Corónica moralizada del Orden de San Agustín en el Perú* [1638]. Edited by Ignacio Prado Pastor. Lima: Universidad Nacional Mayor de San Marcos, Editorial de la Universidad.

Calvo Pérez, Julio

2008   Léxico Quechua. In *Relación de las fábulas y ritos de los incas,* edited by Julio Calvo Pérez and Henrique Urbano, 203–272. Lima: Universidad de San Martín de Porres Press.

Calvo Pérez, Julio, and Henrique Urbano (eds.)

2008   *Relación de las fábulas y ritos de los incas.* Written by Cristóbal de Molina. Lima: Universidad de San Martín de Porres Press.

Castro, Jose Gregorio

1921   Correcciones en la colección de libros y documentos referentes a la historia del Perú de los señores Carlos A. Romero y H. H. Urteaga. *Revista historia* (Lima) 7(1): 17–20.

Ceruti, Constanza

2004   Human bodies as objects of dedication at Inca mountain shrines (northwestern Argentina). *World Archaeology* 36(1): 103–122.

Cieza de León, Pedro de

1976   *The Incas of Pedro Cieza de León* [Part 1, 1553, and Part 2, 1554]. Translated by Harriet de Onís and edited by Victor W. von Hagen. Norman: University of Oklahoma Press.

Cobo, Bernabé

1979   *History of the Inca Empire: An account of the Indians' customs and their origin together with a treatise on Inca legends, history, and social institutions* [1653]. Translated and edited by Roland Hamilton. Austin: University of Texas Press.

1990   *Inca religion and customs* [1653]. Translated and edited by Roland Hamilton. Austin: University of Texas Press.

Cook, Noble David

1981   *Demographic collapse, Indian Peru, 1520–1620.* Cambridge: Cambridge University Press.

1998   *Born to die: Disease and New World conquest, 1492–1650.* Cambridge: Cambridge University Press.

Córdoba Mexía, Pedro de

1925   Información hecha en el Cuzco, por orden del Rey y encargo del Virrey Martín Enríquez acerca de las costumbres que tenían los incas del Perú, antes de la conquista española, en la manera de administrar justicia civil y criminal . . . [1582]. In *Gobernantes del Perú: Cartas y papeles, siglo XVI. Documentos del archivo de Indias,* edited by D. Roberto Levillier, 9: 268–288. Colección de publicaciones históricas de la Biblioteca del Congreso Argentino. Madrid: Imprenta de Juan Pueyo.

Cornejo, Miguel

2002   Sacerdotes y tejedores en la provincia inka de Pachacamac. In *Identidad y transformación en el Tahuantinsuyu y en los Andes coloniales: Perspectivas arqueológicas y etnohistóricas (Primera parte),* edited by Peter Kaulicke, Gary Urton, and Ian Farrington, 171–203. Boletín de arqueología PUCP 6. Lima: Pontificia Universidad Católica del Perú, Fondo Editorial.

Covey, R. Alan

2006   *How the Incas built their heartland: State formation and the innovation of imperial strategies in the Sacred Valley, Peru.* Ann Arbor: University of Michigan Press.

Duviols, Pierre, and César Itier (eds.)

1993   *Relación de antigüedades deste reyno del Pirú.* By Joan de Santa Cruz Pachacuti Yamqui Salcamaygua. Ethnohistoric and linguistic studies by Pierre Duviols and César Itier. Cuzco: Institut Français d'Études Andines, Centro de Estudios Regionales Andinos "Bartolomé de Las Casas."

Esquivel y Navia, Diego de

1980   *Noticias cronológicas de la Gran Ciudad del Cuzco [1749].* Vols. 1 and 2. Edited by Félix Denegri Luna. Lima: Fundación Augusto N. Wiese, Banco, Wiese Ltdo.

Farfán Ayerbe, José María Benigno

1945   Oraciones reconstruidas de Cristóbal de Molina. *Revista del Museo Nacional* (Lima) 14: 72–76

Garcilaso de la Vega, Inca

1960   *Comentarios reales de los incas* [1609]. In *Obras completas del Inca Garcilaso de la Vega.* Biblioteca de autores españoles (continuación), vols. 132–135. Madrid: Ediciones Atlas.

1966   *Royal commentaries of the Incas and general history of Peru, Parts 1 and 2* [1609]. Translated by H. V. Livermore. Austin: University of Texas Press.

Guaman Poma de Ayala, Felipe

1980   *El primer nueva corónica y buen gobierno* [ca. 1615]. Edited by John V. Murra and Rolena Adorno. Translated by Jorge I. Urioste. 3 vols. Mexico City: Siglo Veintiuno.

2009   *The first new chronicle and good government: On the history of the world and the Incas up to 1615.* Translated and edited by Roland Hamilton. Austin: University of Texas Press.

Hampe Martínez, Teodoro

1996   *Cultura barroca y extirpación de idolatrías: La biblioteca de Francisco de Ávila, 1648.* Cuadernos para la Historia de la Reevangelización en América Latina, no. 18. Cuzco: Centro de Estudios Regionales Andinos "Bartolomé de Las Casas."

Heffernan, Ken J.

1996   The mitimaes of Tilka and the Inka incorporation of Chinchaysuyu. *Tawantinsuyu* 2: 23–36.

Hemming, John

1970   *The conquest of the Incas.* New York: Harcourt Brace Jovanovich Press.

The Huarochirí Manuscript: A testament of ancient and colonial Andean religion
[ca. 1608]
1991   Translation from the Quechua by Frank Salomon and George L. Urioste. Austin: University of Texas Press.

Hyslop, John
1990   *Inka settlement planning.* Austin: University of Texas Press.

Levillier, Roberto
1940   *Don Francisco de Toledo, supremo organizador del Perú.* Vol. 2, *Sus informaciones sobre los incas* (1570–1572). Buenos Aires: Espasa-Calpe.

Loayza, Francisco de
1943   Introduction to *Relación de las fábulas y ritos de los incas* [1575], edited by Francisco de Loayza. Los Pequeños Grandes Libros de Historia Americana. Lima: Librería e Imprenta D. Miranda.

MacCormack, Sabine
1991   *Religion in the Andes: Vision and imagination in early colonial Peru.* Princeton, N.J.: Princeton University Press.

Markham, Clements R.
1873   An account of the fables and rites of the Yncas. In *Narratives of the rites and laws of the Yncas.* Translated from the original Spanish manuscripts and edited with notes and an introduction by Clements R. Markham. First series, 48: 1–64. London: Hakluyt Society. Reprinted 1963, 1964, 1969, and 2001.

McEwan, Colin, and Maarten Van de Guchte
1992   Ancestral time and sacred space in Inca state ritual. In *The ancient Americas: Art from sacred landscapes,* edited by Richard F. Townsend, 359–371. Chicago: The Art Institute of Chicago.

Means, Philip Ainsworth
1928   Biblioteca Andina: The chroniclers, or, the writers of the sixteenth and seventeenth centuries who treated of the pre-Hispanic history and culture of the Andean countries. *Transactions of the Connecticut Academy of Arts and Sciences* (New Haven: Connecticut Academy of Arts and Sciences) 29: 271–525.

Meneses, Teodoro L.
1965   Nueva traducción de preces o himnos quechuas del cronista Cristóbal de Molina, el Cusqueño, de *Relación de las fábulas y ritos de los incas. Documenta, Revista de la Sociedad Peruana de Historia* (Lima) 4: 80–111.

Millones, Luis
1964   Un movimiento nativista del siglo XVI: El Taki Onqoy. *Revista Peruana de Cultura* (Lima) 3: 134–140.

2008   Albornoz, Cristóbal de (ca. 1529–ca. 1610). In *Guide to Documentary Sources for Andean Studies, 1530–1900*, edited by Joanne Pillsbury, 2: 21–25. Norman: University of Oklahoma Press.

Millones, Luis (ed.)

1990   *El retorno de las huacas: Estudios y documentos sobre el Taki Onqoy, siglo XVI.* Lima: Instituto de Estudios Peruanos.

Molina, Cristóbal de.

1873   An account of the fables and rites of the Yncas. In *Narratives of the rites and laws of the Yncas*, translated from the original Spanish manuscripts and edited with notes and an introduction by Clements R. Markham. First series, no. 48: 1–64. London: Hakluyt Society. Reprinted 1963, 1964, 1969, and 2001.

1913   Relación de las fábulas y ritos de los incas. Edited by Tomás Thayer Ojeda. *Revista Chilena de Historia y Geografía* (Santiago) 3(5): 117–190.

1916   *Relación de las fábulas y ritos de los incas . . .* Annotations and concordances by Horacio H. Urteaga, biographical and bibliographical information by Carlos A. Romero. Colección de Libros y Documentos Referentes a la Historia del Perú, first series, 1: 1–103. Lima: Sanmartí.

1943   *Fábulas y ritos de los incas . . .* In *Las crónicas de los Molinas.* Biobibliographical prologue by Carlos A. Romero, bibliographical epilogue by Raúl Porras Barrenechea, annotations and short commentaries by Francisco A. Loayza. Los Pequeños Grandes Libros de Historia Americana 1(4): 5–84. Lima: Librería e Imprenta D. Miranda.

1947   *Ritos y fábulas de los incas.* Prologue by Ernesto Morales. Colección Eurindia, no. 2. Buenos Aires: Editorial Futura.

1989   *Relación de las fábulas i ritos de los ingas.* In *Fábulas y mitos de los incas*, edited by Henrique Urbano and Pierre Duviols. Crónicas de América 48: 47–134. Madrid: Historia 16.

2008   *Relación de las fábulas y ritos de los incas.* Edited, with commentary and notes by Julio Calvo Pérez and Henrique Urbano. Lima: Universidad de San Martín de Porres Press.

Morris, Craig, and R. Alan Covey

2003   La plaza central de Huánuco Pampa: Espacio y transformación. In *Identidad y transformación en el Tawantinsuyu y en los Andes coloniales: Perspectivas arqueológicas y etnohistóricas, segunda parte*, edited by Peter Kaulicke, Gary Urton, and Ian Farrington, 133–149. *Boletín de Arqueología PUCP* 7. Lima: Pontificia Universidad Católica del Perú, Fondo Editorial.

Mumford, Jeremy

1998   The Taki Onqoy and the Andean nation: Sources and interpretations. *Latin American Research Review* 33(1): 150–165.

Núñez-Carvallo, Sandro Patrucco

2008   Cabello Valboa, Miguel (ca. 1530–1606). In *Guide to Documentary Sources for Andean Studies, 1530–1900*, 2: 91–94, edited by Joanne Pillsbury. Norman: University of Oklahoma Press.

Ocampo, Baltazar de

1923   Descripción y sucesos históricos de la provincia de Vilcabamba [1610]. Colección de Libros y Documentos Referentes a la Historia del Perú, second series, 7: 151–193. Lima: Sanmartí.

Oré, Luis Jerónimo

1982   *Tercer Concilio Limense, 1582–1583: Versión castellana original de los decretos con el sumario del Segundo Concilio Limense.* Edited and with an introduction by Enrique T. Bartra. Lima: Facultad Pontificia y Civil de Teología de Lima.

1992   *Symbolo Catholico Indiano* [1598]. Lima: Australis.

Ossio, Juan M. A.

2008   Murúa's two manuscripts: A comparison. In *The Getty Murúa*, edited by Thomas B. F. Cummins and Barbara Anderson, 77–94. Los Angeles: Getty Research Institute.

Ossio, Juan M. A. (ed.)

1973   *Ideología Mesiánica del Mundo Andino.* Lima: Prado Pator.

Pachacuti Yamqui Salcamayhua, Juan de Santa Cruz. See Santa Cruz Pachacuti Yamqui Salcamaygua, Joan de.

Polo de Ondegardo, Juan

1916   De los errores y supersticiones de los indios, sacados del tratado y averiguación que hizo el Licenciado Polo [researched ca. 1559; first published in 1585]. Edited by Horacio H. Urteaga. Colección de Libros y Documentos Referentes a la Historia del Perú, first series , 3: 3–43. Lima: Sanmartí.

1965   On the errors and superstitions of the Indians, taken from the treatise and investigation done by Licentiate Polo [researched ca. 1559; first published in 1585]. Translated by A. Brunel, John Murra, and Sidney Muirden, 1–53. New Haven, CT: Human Relations Area Files.

1999   Traslado de un cartapacio a manera de borrador que quedó en los papeles del Licenciado Polo de Ondegardo cerca del linaje de los Ingas y como conquistaron [1572]. In *Polo de Ondegardo: Un cronista vallisoletano en el Perú*, edited by Laura González Pujana, 344–367. Valladolid: Universidad de Valladolid, Instituto de Estudios de Iberoamérica y Portugal.

Porras Barrenechea, Raúl (ed.)

1986   *Los cronistas del Perú (1528–1650).* Lima: Imprenta DESA.

Pizarro, Pedro

1921   *Relation of the discovery and conquest of the kingdoms of Peru* [1571].
       Translated and edited by Philip Ainsworth Means. New York: The
       Cortés Society.

Ramos Gavilán, Alonso

1967   *Historia de Nuestra Señora de Copacabana* [1621]. La Paz: Cámara Na-
       cional de Comercio, Cámara Nacional de Industrias.

Reinhard, Johan

1983   High altitude archaeology and Andean mountain gods. *American Al-
       pine Journal* 25: 54–67.

1985   Sacred mountains: An ethno-archaeological study of high Andean
       ruins. *Mountain Research and Development* 5(4): 299–317.

Rivera Serna, Raúl

1949   Los cuatro Cristóbal de Molina. *Fénix. Revista de la Biblioteca Nacional
       del Perú* (Lima) 6: 590–594.

Rojas, Ricardo

1937   *Himnos quichuas.* Instituto de Literatura Argentina, Vol. 1, No. 11. Bue-
       nos Aires: Facultad de Filosofía y Letras de la Universidad de Buenos
       Aires.

Romero, Carlos A.

1943   *Las crónicas de los Molinas.* Los Pequenos Grandes Libros de Historia
       Americana, Vol. 4. Lima: Librería e Imprenta D. Miranda.

Rostworowski de Diez Canseco, María

1970   Los ayarmaca. *Revista del Museo Nacional* 36: 58–101.

Rowe, John

1946   Inca culture at the time of the Spanish Conquest. In *Handbook of
       South American Indians,* vol. 2, *The Andean civilizations,* edited by Ju-
       lian Steward, 183–330. Bureau of American Ethnology Bulletin, no.
       143. Washington, D.C.: U.S. Government Printing Office.

1953   Eleven Inca prayers from the Zithuwa ritual. *Kroeber Anthropological
       Society Papers* (Berkeley) 8–9: 82–99.

1970   Once oraciones inca del ritual del Zithuwa. Translation by Jorge
       Flores Ochoa, revised and corrected by John H. Rowe and Patricia J.
       Lyon. *Wayka* (Cuzco) 3: 15–33.

1980   Relación de las guacas del Cuzco [1653]. In "An account of the shrines
       of ancient Cuzco," translated and edited by John H. Rowe. *Ñawpa
       Pacha* 17 (1979): 2–80.

Ruiz de Navamuel, Álvaro

1882   La fe y testimonio que va puesta en los cuatro paños . . . (14 January
       1572). In *Informaciones acerca del señorío y gobierno de los ingas hechas*

por mandado de don Francisco de Toledo, edited by Marcos Jiménez de Espada, 16: 245–252. Madrid: Impresa de M. Ginesta.

1940a Información hecha por orden del Virrey Don Francisco de Toledo, con respuestas al mismo interrogatorio utilizado en las cinco informaciones anteriores . . . (19 March–2 June 1571). In *Don Francisco de Toledo, supremo organizador del Perú: Su vida, su obra (1515–1582),* edited by Roberto Levillier, 2: 99–177. Buenos Aires: Espasa-Calpe.

1940b Información hecha en el Cuzco acerca de que los primeros indios sujetados por los incas habitaban en el sitio después por la ciudad y su comarca . . . (4 January–27 February 1572). In *Don Francisco de Toledo, supremo organizador del Perú: Su vida, su obra (1515–1582),* edited by Roberto Levillier, 2: 182–195. Buenos Aires: Espasa-Calpe.

Salomon, Frank

2008 Ávila, Francisco de (ca. 1573–1647). In *Guide to documentary sources for Andean studies, 1530–1900,* edited by Joanne Pillsbury, 2: 58–64. Norman: University of Oklahoma Press.

Santa Cruz Pachacuti Yamqui Salcamaygua, Joan de

1950 Relación de antigüedades deste reyno del Perú [ca. 1613]. In *Tres relaciones de antigüedades peruanas,* edited by Marcos Jiménez de la Espada, 207–281. Asunción, Paraguay: Editora Guaranía.

1993 *Relación de antigüedades deste reyno del Piru* [ca. 1613]. Edited by Pierre Duviols and César Itier. Cuzco: Institut Français d'Études Andines and Centro de Estudios Regionales Andinos "Bartolomé de Las Casas."

Sarmiento de Gamboa, Pedro

2007 *The history of the Incas* [1572]. Translated and edited by Brian S. Bauer and Vania Smith. Introduction by Brian S. Bauer and Jean-Jacques Decoster. Austin: University of Texas Press.

Stanish, Charles, and Brian S. Bauer (eds.)

2004 *Archaeological research on the Islands of the Sun and the Moon, Lake Titicaca, Bolivia: Final results from the Proyecto Tiksi Kjarka.* Los Angeles: Cotsen Institute of Archaeology, University of California.

Stern, Steven J.

1982a *Peru's Indian peoples and the challenge of the Spanish conquest: Huamanga to 1640.* Madison: University of Wisconsin Press.

1982b El Taki Onqoy y la sociedad andina (Huamanga, siglo XVI). *Allpanchis* (Cuzco) 19: 49–77.

Thayer Ojeda, Tomás

1920 Las biografías de los dos "Cristóbales de Molina" publicadas por el escritor peruano don Carlos A. Romero. *Revista Chilena de Historia y Geografía* (Santiago) 36: 1–46.

Timberlake, Marie

2008 Provincial councils of Lima: Texts and images. In *Guide to documentary sources for Andean studies, 1530–1900*, edited by Joanne Pillsbury, 1: 197–208. Norman: University of Oklahoma Press.

Toledo, Francisco de

1943 Nomination letter of Cristóbal de Molina to the position of General Inspector for the Cuzco parishes (4 November 1575). In *Las crónicas de los Molinas*, edited by Carlos Romero, Appendix A, xxii–xxiv. Lima: Librería e Imprenta D. Miranda.

Urbano, Henrique

1990 Cristóbal de Molina, el Cusqueño: Negocios eclesiásticos, mesianismo y Taqui Onqoy. *Revista Andina* 8(1): 265–283.

2008a Ediciones de la "Relación." In *Relación de las fábulas y ritos de los incas*, written by Cristóbal de Molina; edited by Julio Calvo Pérez and Henrique Urbano, lxxix–lxxx. Lima: Universidad de San Martín de Porres Press.

2008b Introducción a la vida y obra de Cristóbal de Molina. In *Relación de las fábulas y ritos de los incas*, written by Cristóbal de Molina; edited by Julio Calvo Pérez and Henrique Urbano, xi–lxvi. Lima: Universidad de San Martín de Porres Press.

2008c Molina, Cristóbal de (ca. 1529–1585). In *Guide to documentary sources for Andean studies, 1530–1900*, edited by Joanne Pillsbury, 2: 427–428. Norman: University of Oklahoma Press.

Urbano, Henrique, and Pierre Duviols (eds.)

1989 *Fábulas y mitos de los incas*. Madrid: Historia 16.

Urton, Gary D.

1981 *At the crossroads of the earth and the sky: An Andean cosmology*. Austin: University of Texas Press.

Vasco de Contreras y Valverde, Dean

1982 *Relación de la ciudad del Cusco* [1649]. Prologue and transcription by María del Carmen Martín Rubio. Cuzco: Imprenta Amauta.

Wachtel, Nathan

1977 *The vision of the vanquished: The Spanish Conquest of Peru through Indian eyes, 1530–1570*. New York: Barnes and Noble Press.

Wiener, Charles

1880 *Pérou et Bolivie: Récit de voyage suivi d'études archéologiques et ethnographiques et de notes sur l'écriture et les langues des populations indiennes*. Paris: Hachette et Cie.

Zuidema, R. Tom

1964 *The ceque system of Cuzco: The social organization of the capital of the*

Inca. Translated by Eva M. Hooykaas. International Archives of Ethnography, supplement to vol. 50. Leiden: E. J. Brill.

1973 Kinship and ancestor cult in three Peruvian communities: Hernández Príncipe's account in 1622. *Bulletin de l'Institut Français d'Études Andines* 2(1): 16–23.

1982 Catachillay: The role of the Pleiades and of the Southern Cross and ∂ and ß Centauri in the calendar of the Incas. In *Ethnoastronomy and archaeoastronomy in the American Tropics*, edited by A. F. Aveni and G. Urton, 203–229. New York: Annals of the New York Academy of Sciences, vol. 385.

Zuidema, R. Tom, and Gary Urton

1976 La Constelación de la Llama en los Andes peruanos. *Allpanchis* (Cuzco) 9: 59–119.

INDEX

Acahuara (place), 25, 26
Acarí, area of, xxviii, 87
Achicoc, 18
Acoyapongo (place), 32, 33, 59
Aepiran (hill), 25
Albornoz, Cristóbal, xi, xii, xviii,
    xxii–xxv, xxix, xxxii, 94nn10,15,
    97n4, 102nn56,59, 114nn156,157,
    119n17, 120n16
Amaybamba (place), 43, 107n111
Anaguarque (hill), 59, 60, 113n150,
    114n157
Ancasmarca (town), 12–13, 97nn19,23
Andahuaylillas (town), 33, 100n33,
    103nn65,66
Anta (town), 77
Antahuayla (shrine), 25, 26, 32, 33,
    100n33, 103n65
Antisuyo, 12, 32, 34, 39, 77
Apcaras (province), xxiv
Apin Punchao (statue), 37
Apotin Uiracochan (shrine), 43
Apu Mayta (kin group), 103n68
Apurimac (river), 33, 34
Arayraca (kin group), 33, 103n69
Arco de la Plata, location of, 117n188
Arequipa (city), xii, xviii, xxii, xxiv,
    xxvii, 84, 94n15, 102n16
Atahualpa, rule of, 95n3

Ataorupaqui, xxvi
Atun (kin group), 33
Atun Uiracochan (shrine), 43
Aucaylla (kin group), 34, 104n76
Aucaypata (place), 30
Auraba (place), 60
Ávila, Francisco de, vii, xii, xiii
Ayacucho, xxix, xxxii, 94n10. *See also*
    Huamanga
Ayarcache, xix, xx, 80, 119n14
Ayarmaca (town), 51, 109n127
Ayascay, birth rite, xv, 69, 75

Bobadilla, Isabel de, house of, 31

Cabello Valboa, Miguel, xii, xx,
    94n9, 95n2, 96nn6,7, 98nn3,6,
    115n160
Cachagaes, 81, 82
Cacha Uiracdocha (place), 25, 26
Cachona (town), 60, 113n151
Cajamarca, ix
Calancha, Antonio de la, xxvii
Calispuquio (spring), 115n164
Calix Puquio, 64
Calpariçu, 18
Camascas, 18, 19
Cañari, origin myth of, xxv, xxvi, 11,
    12, 96n15, 97nn16–18

145

Capac (kin group), 33, 103n69
Capacocha, ritual of, xv, 77–83, 107n114, 108n121, 118nn1,2
Capac Uilca (place), 25, 26
Capi Mayo (river), 69
Caquia Xaquixaguana, site of, 98n7
Cargo Cults, xxxii
Chanca Uiracochan (shrine), 43
Chaueticuzco (kin group), 33
Chaullay (town), 107n109
Chavin Cuzco (kin group), 103n69
Chicha, ix, xxx, 11, 28, 31, 39, 48, 51, 52, 54, 58, 60–62, 66, 69, 86, 87, 89, 102n60, 107n100, 113n148
Chima (kin group), 34, 104n81
Chinchasuyo, 32, 39, 77
Chita (place), 33, 59
Chitapampa (place), 104n77
Choco (town), 60, 113n151
Chota (place), 34
Chuquicaca (city), 84
Chuquicancha (place), 59, 79, 80, 119n10
Chuquichaca (bridge), 43, 107n109
Chuquichanca Uiracochan (shrine), 44
Chuquiylla, 31, 37, 80. See also Thunder
Churicalla (place), 33, 34
Cieza de León, Pedro, 96nn4,11, 101n47, 102n59
Cinchi Roca, 111n138
Citua, ritual of, xv, 30–50
Coca, 25, 28, 30, 70, 89, 112n144
Collasuyo, 31–33, 39, 77
Collopata (place), 25, 26, 100n20
Condors, stone figures of, 5
Copacabana (town), 111n144
Copper, objects made of, 19, 60, 97n18

Coricancha, 16, 21, 23, 24, 30, 31, 54, 97n5, 102n54
Coya Pacssa, figure of, 37
Creator God, 17, 20, 21, 23, 27, 30, 31, 34, 36–39, 41–49, 51, 57, 60–63, 67, 71, 78, 81, 89, 98n6; actions of, 5–11; fields of, 72; house and statue of, 15, 68, 77; priests of, 65, 66, 78. See also Viracocha
Crus Moqo (place), 100n36
Cullupata (place), 25
Cuntisuyo, 32, 34, 77
Cusibamba (place), 33, 34, 104n85
Cusicayo, xxvi
Cuti (place), 25, 26
Cuycusa (kin group), 33, 103n68
Cuyos (ethnic group), 13, 34, 104n79

Drums, 4, 63, 115n163

Eagle, stone figure of, 43
Earth, worship of, 47, 48, 80
Enríquez, Martín, xviii

Flood, myths of, 4, 5, 11, 12, 20, 60, 97n21

García de Castro, Lope, xxii, xxxi, 87, 120nn16,18
Ghost Dance, xxxii
Gold, objects made of, 23, 27, 28, 37–39, 41, 50, 56, 58, 60, 62, 63, 65, 66, 70, 77, 81, 89, 112n146, 114n157, 115n163
Guacapanco Maio (river), 69
Guamancancha (hill), 61, 114n156
Guarachico, male initiation rite, 50, 51, 69, 109n132, 111n144
Guasca (sacred rope), 68, 117n181

Hanan Cuzco, 16, 39, 48, 61, 63, 66, 67, 106n97, 107n103, 116n174

Hatun (kin group), 103n69

Haucaypata, ix, 16, 28, 57, 61, 69, 77, 101n44

Hawk, 60, 71; stone figures of, 5, 43, 62

Hospital for the Natives (Cuzco), xi, xiv, xvi, xxxiv, 1

Huacamaya, 11, 12, 69, 97n18

Huacarpay (place), 103n64

Huacayñan (hill), xxvi, 11, 12

Huamanga, xi, xviii, xxii, xxiv, xxix, xxxii, 84, 88, 120n16

Huanacauri (mountain), ix, xx, 17, 23, 26, 37, 38, 41, 48, 51, 52, 55, 59, 80, 98n13, 99n9, 111n138, 114n157, 119n14; fields of, 72

Huánuco (city), 88

Huaraypacha (place), 33

Huarivilca (shrine), 8, 96n10

Huaro (town), 19, 20, 32, 98n9, 99n10, 107n110

Huasano (hill), xxvi

Huascar Inca, xvii, 1, 62, 95n3, 117n181

Huayllacan (ethnic group), 104n79

Huayna Capac, xvii, xxxiv, 1, 95n3, 117n181

Huayna Punchao, statue of, 66

Huaypar (place), 32, 33

Huaypon (place), 44, 107n112

Huhuanina (kin group), 103n68

Hurin Cuzco, 16, 32, 39, 48, 61, 63, 66, 67, 106n97, 107n103, 116n174

Inca Oillo, statue of, 27, 37, 100n40

Jaquejahuana. *See* Xaquixahuana

Jauja (region), 8, 94n17, 120n18

Juturoma (place), 25, 100n29

La Paz (city), 84

La Raya (place), 25, 100n22

Lartaún, Sebastián, xii, xiv–xix, xxi, xxviii, xxxiv, 1, 95nn1,2, 119n15, 119n1

Lightning, 18, 23

Lima, 84; Third Provincial Council of, xii, xvii–xviii, xx, xxiv, 95n1

Limapampa, 16, 30

Limatambo (town), 103n75

Litters, travel by, 27, 50

Loarte, Gabriel de, xxv

López de Segovia, Hernán, house of, 15, 97n5

Lucanas (province), xxiv

Lurucache (place), 25, 100n24

Mamaconas, 26

Mama Huaco, cult of, 72

Manco Capac, ix, xix, xx, 4, 6, 51, 62, 63, 98n13, 109n129, 111n138; sister of, 72

Manco Inca, xvii, xxxi, 1, 43, 95n3, 119n4

Mantucalla, 26, 28, 59, 100n38

Maras (ethnic group), 33, 62, 96n7, 103n68, 109n127

Marcahuasi (place), 34, 103nn72,73

Markham, Clements, vii, xiii, xx, xxxv, 91

Masca (kin group), 34, 104n81

Matahua (hill), 55, 59, 111n138

Mauro Pancunco, straw balls called, 35, 36

Mitimas, ix, 4, 32–34

Mollebamba (place), 25, 26, 100n31

Moon, in calendar, 21, 30, 67, 99n2, 105n89, 117n179; fields of, 72; origin of, 6, 8; priests of, 65, 66; role within statue of, 54, 68, 77; wor-

ship of, 20, 37, 48, 55, 57, 60–63, 80, 89, 111n137
Moro Orco, house of, 68
Moto (hill), 25, 99n15
Mullu, ix, 25, 30, 77, 81, 86, 88
Mummies: of Inca kings and queens, 36–40, 52, 63, 67, 68, 69, 106n92; of Mama Huaco, 72

Ocampo, Baltazar, xxvii
Olivera, Luis de, xi, xxviii–xxxii, 84, 87, 94nn12,16, 119n1, 120nn5,9
Ollantaytambo (town), 43, 70, 71, 117n186
Oma (town), 50, 108n125
Omoto Yanacauri (place), 25, 26
Origin myth: of Ancasmarca, 12; of the Cañari, 11; of the Incas, 4–11
Ortiz de Guzmán, Diego de, house of, 15, 97n5

Pacaritambo (place), xix, 7, 47, 56, 80, 96n7, 100n41, 108n115, 111n140, 118n14
Pachacamac (shrine), xxx, 8, 85, 120n10
Pachacuti Inca Yupanqui, xv, xx, 14–17, 50, 62, 63, 69, 76, 94nn7,8; calendar system, 14; creates Sun worship, 15; vision of Creator God, 16, 17, 97n3, 98nn6,12, 117n181
Pachayachachi, 8, 15, 21
Palpasillo, statue of, 27, 37, 100n39
Parinacocha, xi, xxviii, xxix, 84, 94n15
Pati (place), 25, 26
Paullo (town and ethnic group), 34, 104n79
Picchu (hill), 114n157
Pisac (town and river), 32–34, 104nn78–80

Pizarro, Francisco de, xxix, xxx, 85, 95n3, 120n11
Pomacanchi (place), 100n21
Poquen Cancha (sun temple), 4
Pucara (town), 8, 96n11
Puma Chupa, location of, 16, 70, 71, 117nn184,186
Pumamarca (place), 31
Pumas, skins of, 63, 115nn161,163
Punchao Inca, statue of, 21
Puquin (hill), 59, 66, 95n1

Queros Huanacauri (place), 25, 26
Quesco (kin group), 34
Quicochico (female initiation rite), 69, 75, 76, 118n5
Quihuares (town), 100n19
Quilliya Colca (hill), 59
Quipus, xv, xxi, 14, 97n1; keepers of, 78, 82
Quiquijana (river), 33, 100n30, 103nn66,67
Quirasmanta, ravine of, 56
Quishuarcancha, house of the Creator, 15, 16, 31, 97n4, 102n55
Quispicanchi (place), 25, 26, 100n36
Quito (province), xxvi, 11, 19
Quizco (kin group), 104n81

Racchi (town), 9, 96n11, 100nn26,27
Ramos Gavilán, Alonso, 99n6, 115n162
Rauaraya (shrine), 114n155
Raurau (kin group), 34, 104n81
Rauraua (place), 58, 59, 113n152
Rimacpampa, 101n50
Rondocan (place), 25, 100n18
Rontoca (place), 25, 26
Ruiz de Navamuel, Álvaro, xvii, xxi, xxv, 96n2

Rumi Huasi Bajo, location of, 119n10
Rurucache (place), 25, 26
Ruruoma (place), 25, 26
Rutuchico (first hair cutting), 69, 75, 118n3

Sacalpiña (place), 77
Sanco, paste of, 36, 37, 41, 48, 49, 106n90, 107n102
San Juan, ritual of, 101n53
Sañoc (kin group), 34, 104n76
San Sebastián (town), 79
Santo Domingo, church of, 30, 54
Saphi (river), 117n183
Sarmiento de Gamboa, Pedro; xi, xvii, xviii, xxi, xxv, xxvi, 95n2, 96nn4,6,7,11,15, 97n15, 98nn6,8, 98n3, 101n53
Satpina (place), 33, 34, 118n3
Sausiro, field of, 72
Shamans, 18
Sicuani (town), 100n25
Silver, objects made of, 19, 27, 28, 50, 62, 63, 65, 66, 70, 77, 81, 89, 112n146
Sinchi Roca, rule of, 63, 115n160
Solstice celebrations, xv
Soras (province), xxiv
Sorcerers, xv, 18–20, 88, 89
Stars, 12, 89, 97n24; origin of, 6, 8
Sucanca (place), 25, 26
Succanca (place), 25, 26, 100n37
Sucsu (kin group), 104n76
Sun: fields of, 72, 89; origin of, 6, 8, 45; Pachacuti's vision of, 16, 17; priest of, 31, 57, 60, 65, 69, 79; statue of, 36, 37, 54, 66, 68, 77; worship of, 4, 15, 20, 21, 26, 38, 39, 41, 42, 47–49, 51, 53, 55, 57, 61–63
Sunto (place), 25, 26
Susurpuquio, 16, 59, 98n6

Sutic (kin group), 33, 103n68
Sutuc (place), 25

Tambotoco (cave), xix, 28, 62, 98n13, 100n41, 119n14
Tantar (place), 33, 34, 104n84
Taqui Onqoy, ix, xv, xxiii, xxiv, xxviii–xxxiii, 84–88, 94n10
Tarpuntaes, ix, 23, 26, 28, 30, 55, 60, 74
Tarpuntai, ayllu of, 34, 104n76
Thunder, 98n11; fields of, 72; priests of, 65, 66; worship of, 17, 18, 23, 30, 36, 39, 41, 42, 48, 49, 51, 54, 55, 57, 60–63, 68, 77, 79
Tiahuanaco, site of, xxv, 10, 20, 48, 96n4
Tilca (place), 33, 34, 103n72
Titicaca: island, 6, 7, 8, 27; lake, xxv, xxx; shrine, 85, 103n60, 120n10
Tocapo Viracocha, 7, 10
Toledo, Francisco, xi, xii, xvi, xx, xxiv, xxv–xxviii, xxxiv, 85, 95n3, 120n8, 121n19
Toro, Pedro de, 87
Tunas, use of, 116n174
Tupac Amaro, xi, xvii, xxvi, xxvii, 95n3, 120nn8,19

Uicaquicao (kin group), 33
Uirapiricoc, 18
Urcos (town), 43, 100n32, 107n110
Urcos Viracocha (place), 25, 26
Uro (kin group), 33, 103n69
Urusayua (shrine), 43
Uscaymata, ayllo de, 33, 103n68
Usño, 31, 39, 102n59

Vasco de Contreras y Valverde, Dean, xii, xvi, xvii, xx, xxi, 95n2
Vicaquirao (kin group), 103n69

Vilcabamba (province), ix, xvi, xxvi, xxvii, xxxi, 84, 85, 88, 95n3, 107n109, 120nn4–8, 121n19

Vilcanota (place and river), 25, 26, 104nn79,80

Viracocha (Creator God), xxv, 31, 43, 96n11, 97nn3,4, 100nn27,32, 107n110, 110n135

Viracocha Inca, 16

Viracochan (place), 25, 100n32, 107n110

Xaquixahuana (place), 33, 103n71

Xusçu (kin group), 34

Yacalla Huaca (place), 25, 26

Yacarcaes, 19

Yahuaymin (kin group), 33

Yanapampa (place), 25

Yana Yana (place), 25, 26, 100n21

Yapomayho (kin group), 33

Yauira (hill), 59, 61, 62

Yauraba (hill), 61

Yaurisque (town), 33, 34, 104nn82,83

Ymaymana Viracocha, 7, 10